The
Kaurs
of
1984

Advance Praise for *The Kaurs of 1984*

'Graphic, disturbing and searing, this account of the untold stories of women caught in the violence of 1984 brings to light much that lay in plain sight, and was yet wilfully unseen. It also points to the long legacies that histories of violence and trauma carry, and the increasingly urgent need for societies, indeed for us in India, to find a way not only to heal such wounds, but also to work towards justice for the survivors and the memories of those they lost.'

—**Urvashi Butalia, feminist publisher and author of** *The Other Side of Silence: Voices from the Partition of India*

'The state-organized genocide against the Sikh community in 1984 was a watershed event in our history and yet it was completely covered up. Today, in its fortieth anniversary year, there is still too little done—too little justice; too little known; too little written of something so enormous. Sanam's book is a welcome, powerful, courageous and unique perspective of this entire period through the lens of those who bore the most brutal brunt of it—the Kaurs. A must-read.'

— **Shonali Bose, film-maker**

'The anti-Sikh pogrom of November 1984, in Delhi and other cities of India, unleashed forces whose impact was felt, especially in Punjab, for a long time. In addition to being witnesses to gruesome murders of their loved ones, Sikh women became victims of ruthless rapes by marauding crowds let loose by the agencies that were supposed to protect their lives and honour. Having lost the breadwinners of their families, these women

had to fend for the surviving members. From that point of view, Sanam's *The Kaurs of 1984* has filled a void in portraying the plight of such women.'
>   —**G.B.S. Sidhu, former special secretary, R&AW, and author of *The Khalistan Conspiracy***

'The unheard voices of the Sikh women of 1984—some murdered, some alive to bear witness, some rape survivors and some of them militants themselves. This book gathers their experiences with sensitivity, commitment, historical responsibility and a deep sense of justice, shaped as the author is by his own experience in human rights work and his rootedness in the community.'
>   —**Nivedita Menon, professor, Jawaharlal Nehru University**

'Sanam Sutirath Wazir has spent the last decade researching the anti-Sikh pogrom of 1984 and its fallout on communities that have received neither justice nor closure. The lived experience of the pogrom's survivors recorded here is vital to our understanding of the events. Having worked with Sanam for several years while he campaigned and mobilized on this issue, I was witness to the exceptional quality of his work and his deeply felt interest in the cause, and this book is a reflection of it.'
>   —**Aakar Patel, chair, Amnesty International India**

The
Kaurs
of
1984

THE UNTOLD, UNHEARD
STORIES OF SIKH WOMEN

Sanam Sutirath Wazir

HarperCollins *Publishers* India

First published in India by HarperCollins *Publishers* 2024
4th Floor, Tower A, Building No. 10, DLF Cyber City,
DLF Phase II, Gurugram, Haryana – 122002
www.harpercollins.co.in

2 4 6 8 10 9 7 5 3 1

Copyright © Sanam Sutirath Wazir 2024

P-ISBN: 978-93-6213-029-7
E-ISBN: 978-93-6213-817-0

The views and opinions expressed in this book are the author's own and the facts are as reported by him, and the publishers are not in any way liable for the same.

Sanam Sutirath Wazir asserts the moral right to be identified as the author of this work.

All rights reserved. No part of this publication may be reproduced, stored in a retrieval system, or transmitted, in any form or by any means, electronic, mechanical, photocopying, recording or otherwise, without the prior permission of the publishers.

Typeset in 11.5/16 Minion Pro by
Manipal Technologies Limited, Manipal

Printed and bound at
Replika Press Pvt. Ltd.

This book is produced from independently certified FSC® paper to ensure responsible forest management.

To all the victims of the anti-Sikh massacre of 1984 and to all those innocents who were tortured or killed during the violence in Punjab.

*To my parents, Surinder Kaur and Late Tirath Singh Wazir—
it's impossible to thank you for what you have done for me.
And,
my nani, Late Pritam Kaur.*

Contents

	Foreword	xi
	Introduction	xix
1.	Saka Neela Tara—Operation Blue Star	1
2.	Chaurasi ki Na Insafi	37
3.	Sultanpuri	48
4.	Raj Nagar	56
5.	Mukherjee Nagar	63
6.	Hondh	65
7.	November 1984	69
8.	From Pens to Guns	88
9.	Militant Bride	107
10.	The Daughter of a Cop	116
11.	Letters from Jail	139
12.	Widows in Delhi	158
	Epilogue	173
	Acknowledgements	217
	Notes	221

Foreword

In my memory of post-independent India, 1984 marks the most gruesome violence that was unleashed upon a community, in this case the Sikhs, who were killed right in the capital of the nation in full view of the government of the day, with no recourse to relief from the police, the civil administration, or the army which was stationed just a few kilometres from Rashtrapati Bhawan that housed the head of state, the President of India, Gyani Zail Singh, himself a Sardar. The shock of that violence which I witnessed in 1984 came to overlay the violence of the Partition riots that I, as a child of six, had witnessed in Delhi in 1947 and had never left me. So I understood the anguish of the Sikhs who have never forgotten the violence of 1984 that was so unexpected and so overwhelming that it has remained a moment of great betrayal.

Foreword

'*Humko apne watan ke logon ne hi maara!* (We were killed by our own countrypeople!)' has been permanently etched in our collective social memory.

The year 1984 has become etched in the collective social memory of not only the Sikhs but of citizens' groups, civil rights groups and women's groups as it led to a massive response from civil society: groups like the Nagrik Ekta Manch, Citizens for Democracy, students and teachers of Delhi University began to visit relief camps, as did journalists who had swung into action even before curfew was lifted. And as they did their work, knowledge of the enormity of the killings, the virtual slaughter in particular colonies and the deliberate breakdown of law and order by the police agencies added to the widespread rioting and arson that had dominated the streets as well as the genocidal targeting of the Sikhs whose homes were invaded and where Sikh men were dragged out and systematically killed, using techniques which clearly showed a preparation for the assaults. It was in this backdrop that the People's Union for Democratic Rights (PUDR), the democratic rights group of which I was a member, began to compile a report on the violence we had all witnessed. That report, titled 'Who Are the Guilty?' became a sort of landmark in report writing. The report was compiled in a record seventeen days and it made clear that the riots had been organized by the party in power and the government of the day. While the government went on to deny the substance of the report, one critical consequence of the report was that the public sphere and the Sikh community did not treat the killings as a Hindu–Sikh riot, but one where the state had unleashed violence upon a particular community. This was pointed out to me by a Sikh lawyer friend from Punjab who said that the report was critical in shaping the immediate present and future in terms of acknowledging the critical work of democratic rights groups which governments and political parties give little credit for.

The first act of documenting the violence was a necessary pre-condition for taking the fact-finding report into the public domain in order to substantiate the fact of the violence itself. As the report was assembled with frenetic zeal, due to round-the-clock work of a group of people in the PUDR to get affidavits from journalists and others, Sumanto Banerjee, a journalist himself, came up with the powerful title 'Who Are the Guilty?'. When the press conference was held on 17 November, the government was forced to rebut the substance of the report, but in the public sphere the report stayed as the first record of state complicity: in a sense the archive on 1984 had already begun to be compiled. Eyewitness accounts were cited and thereafter everything that archivists sought to record had already made a beginning. There were many other reports that also appeared in the weeks that followed but, more importantly, detailed reports began to make an appearance. As more and more people, citizens' groups and relief workers, and women's movement activists interacted with those who had been targeted by the mobs they also informally started collecting accounts of what had happened, the names of people killed, houses destroyed, property looted, those who were wounded, the women who were widowed and left destitute as the main breadwinners of the families had been killed.

I am not sure what has happened to all the information compiled in those days or whether any of that material ended up in any archive; I have a small archive of such papers, but there must be so much that has gone unrecorded or unarchived. Apart from the paper trail, there are the unrecorded and undocumented memories that people have carried in their heads which will soon be lost because those carrying the memories are getting older and will one day pass away. It is therefore critical to make a concerted effort to collect these memories, as Sanam has sought to complete in this critical book of oral accounts of those who bore witness to the terror of 1984, not just of the November killings but also the violence and killings entailed by Operation Blue Star.

What Sanam is now doing was preceded by what Nandita Haksar and a group of six recorders and I did in the beginning of 1985 and carried on for few intense months by recording the eyewitness accounts of those who were targeted in the attacks, occasionally those who were named as part of the violent mobs and those who provided relief and support work over the many months of 1985. There were literally hundreds of accounts that were compiled—many more were carried in the heads of volunteers and peace activists. Some made their way into published articles and books; special issues, like the one brought out by *Manushi*, which documented the violence as also rapes, have mostly been swept under the carpet by scholars. Ram Rehman was among the first photographers to go to Trilokpuri, the scene of some of the most gruesome killings. He captured the tragedy of 1984: stunned and grieving women, burnt homes and the occasional Sikh male survivor shorn of his hair and his turban, weeping as Pramila Dandavate wiped his tears. These images are permanently etched in my memory. Years later, Gauri Gill created another archive of photographs of women and children who were survivors of 1984, with texts written by a select group of people who had engaged with 1984 that evocatively spoke to the visual images Gauri had created.

Even before the curfew was lifted, the first peace marches had happened as concerned citizens took out processions in colonies where hostile crowds of arsonists still had control of the streets. They went to Trilokpuri, the site of horrifying violence and found deserted streets with only a few half-crazed souls cowering in fear. Later, Dilip Simeon, a colleague from Delhi University, recalled an event which he has never forgotten, of a child in her mother's arms crying out in fear as she saw a group of people coming towards them: '*Meri ma ko mat marna!* (Don't kill my mother!)' She thought another attack was imminent—that is what groups of men did to innocent people and I wonder if she has ever been able to get over the fear she experienced in 1984.

We all had such memories. During the course of our visits to the colonies in the periphery of Delhi (where the poor had been relocated during the clean-up of the city—masterminded by Indira Gandhi's son during the Emergency—that had supposedly made them the proud possessors of 25-square-yard plots, upon which they had built their homes, and which we middle class Delhi-ites saw for the first time in our lives), we would come across people or stories that would move us in particular ways. In Garhi in South Delhi, I saw a three-year-old girl who looked mutely at us: she had lost her speech after the attacks in her area had killed her father who had been a vegetable vendor. Her face continues to haunt me to date and I do not know if she ever recovered her speech. Another young woman of about eighteen or nineteen lost her husband in the attacks. She had been married for less than a year and was a few months pregnant in November 1984. The shock had resulted in a miscarriage. This young woman's story made such an impact on me that I went and pleaded with the only Sikh businessman I knew at that time to give her a job so that she could be financially rehabilitated. Though he was sympathetic to her plight he thought I was a bit touched in the head myself: he couldn't give her a job as he ran a truck business, an all-male enterprise if ever there was one. He gave me some money instead for the relief work we were doing.

For years afterwards, and even to this day, I come across stories of 1984. It's like an undercurrent in the life of Delhi. You get into a cab or go to a certain kind of gathering and say 'Where were you when 1984 happened' and people will tell you their stories—of landing at airports and being hidden, of hair being cut, of getting home to hear more accounts of relatives being killed, of acts of great brutality and, occasionally, of great generosity. Perhaps it was these stories and the need to counter the state narrative on 1984 that led to my obsession with archiving the voices of the living present. I kept talking about it to everyone until Nandita Haksar, my student from Miranda House and by 1984 a young lawyer, said: 'Okay, then let's do it.' She got hold of a couple of tape recorders and a few cassettes, and we formed ourselves into a group of people who began the process of documenting 1984. It took us three years to collect the narratives, transcribe and translate them, find a publisher, put in money into the publication and then bring the work out. It was published as *The Delhi Riots: Three Days in the Life of a Nation*. 'Three days in the life of a nation' became so voluminous that finally Nandita and I had to leave out some of the interviews that we had conducted, and these missing interviews are now part of my personal archive. It is part of a collection of many other papers—newspaper cuttings, lists of people killed or missing which we had compiled on our visits to the colonies where the worst attacks had taken place, some photographs, and sundry other bits among which only yesterday I found a small piece written by another student, Shonali Bose: an account of a play we had created on 1984 which had got lost among my pile of papers.

Sanam's book *The Kaurs of 1984*, through its narratives, picks up on many threads opened but not fully explored to date. It includes for the first time, in my knowledge, the terrible violence suffered by women caught in the vortex of happenings which were not of their making; women who were in the Golden Temple when Operation Blue Star was launched in June 1984; and women who were mourning for Indira Gandhi on the morning of 1 November because they were her supporters—she had given them plots of land that made them independent homeowners for the first time. Some were even observing a fast. But they were mercilessly killed nevertheless. The first narrator, Nanki Bai, in our book described the rapes of young girls, powerfully recorded by Sanam too in his book which begins with an account of sexual violence which itself is remarkable because there is a veil of silence around sexual violence in 1984. Academics would not acknowledge it because it would indict 'Hindu' men which was inconvenient for them; the Sikh community by and large did not address it and even the commission reports buried it—neither the Misra Commission nor the Nanavati Commission paid any attention to the FIRs that were filed. In the powerful *Manushi* report, in Issue No. 25, sexual violence features and is available on the *Manushi* website, but not everyone goes to websites.

Foreword

Oral history, however, has a way of bringing out inconvenient truths and Sanam has done just that; women cannot be silenced when they are given a chance to tell their stories as they have lived it. This book is a must-read for those who believe in justice and want to reach out to the anguished souls of the survivors whose lives were irretrievably shattered by mobs who were unleashed upon them. 1984 must never be forgotten—not now, not ever.

April 2024 **Uma Chakravarti**

Introduction

'There is no short cut or simple prescription for healing the wounds and divisions of a society in the aftermath of sustained violence ... It is, however, an essential one to address in the process of building a lasting peace. Examining the painful past, acknowledging it and understanding it ... each society must discover its own route to reconciliation. Reconciliation cannot be imposed from outside, nor can someone else's map get us to our destination: it must be our own solution ...'[1]

—Archbishop Desmond Tutu

In 2014, Amnesty International asked me to research the Sikh massacre of 1984, which had wreaked havoc across north India, especially in New Delhi where over 3,000 people were

Introduction

killed. The official numbers seem to cast only a partial shadow on the true magnitude of the tragedy. Lingering whispers allude to a toll surpassing official acknowledgement. As with distressing narratives, the victims here too are not mere statistics, but men, women and children who confronted the searing grasp of torment. Women, particularly, shouldered the burden of this unforgiving reality, their stories indelibly marked by harrowing scars.

Amidst reverberations of sorrow, the postlude materializes akin to a disjointed reverie. Thousands, forcibly uprooted from their abodes, drift like forlorn spirits in search of sanctuary. Among this displaced throng, at least 50,000[2] individuals find precarious solace within the confines of relief camps that blur the boundary between despair and hope in a delicate choreography of survival. Orchestrated after the assassination of Indira Gandhi, the then prime minister of India, by her Sikh bodyguards, the massacre took place six years before I was born.

I had read about the victims of the anti-Sikh massacre and the mind-numbing cruelties they faced in the aftermath of the violence—from the slow judicial response to the horrific stories of how political machinations had enabled and empowered the perpetrators. Myriad books have been written about the massacre, and during my time with Amnesty International, I read nearly all of them along with nine judicial reports on the subject. But a few months into my field work I realized that a crucial perspective on this bloodied epoch in modern Indian history was almost entirely missing. The voices of the women—the Kaurs of 1984—were silent in the existing narrative.

Introduction

The Kaurs of 1984 are women who were random victims in the lottery of the state machinery. They are women who took up arms, who stood by their militant men and who were, at one point in time in their lives, militants themselves. They are survivors of rape. They are among those who were murdered. They are the ones who saw hell coming to life with the securitization of the state a few months after Operation Blue Star and the massacre, when armed police personnel made their presence felt on every street, lane and by-lane, crowding around the entrance of the Golden Temple complex, and of colleges and shops. They saw houses getting raided in the middle of the night and entire lives getting destroyed in a matter of hours. In this unending chaos, and with the passage of time since then, the voices of the Kaurs who lived through unimaginable horror and trauma have been silenced. And once I became aware of this silence, I wanted to undo it. I wanted to ensure that the voices of these survivors were heard and their stories remembered.

I travelled extensively through Amritsar, Gurdaspur, Tarn Taran, Patiala, Sangrur, Ludhiana, Moga, Bathinda, Ropar, Faridkot, Ferozepur, Kapurthala, Sangrur Hoshiarpur, Kanpur and Delhi to meet survivors and activists, and record their personal accounts. I met dozens of Sikh women during this period—all of them victims of the violence, all of them mostly ignored by the state and the media. They are legion: a father's favourite daughter, forced into militancy after her father was burnt alive in front of her; a young wife trapped in the Golden Temple as the army stormed in, holding on to her dead child for three days; trapped after a pilgrimage to the Golden Temple, a college student is forbidden from returning home—her father's desperate plea reveals the unsettling truth: her elder sister had already been rounded by security personnel. Most of the personal stories included in this book are stories that I heard while interviewing these people. Some, however, have been reproduced from the affidavits the women filed with the various enquiry commissions that were set up after the anti-Sikh massacre.

In 2016, I received a few copies of the reports made by some of these enquiry commissions and committees through an RTI application. For quite a few of the other commissions and committees, however, there were no records of their reports and findings. It was a tedious process. When I visited the Delhi secretariat for the first time, I took photocopies of the reports with me and upon seeing them, the official in charge asked me, 'Why do you want these reports? All these people have been fairly compensated and are living a good life. What do you want to do now?'

I was not shocked by this question, at least not as much as I had thought I would be. After all, Darshan Kaur (a survivor of the 1984 anti-Sikh violence, among those interviewed by the author) had told me a similar story about how everyone, from bank officials to people in their workplaces, had bullied them for receiving compensations and for getting jobs. What no one acknowledged was the fact that in spite of the compensations and the jobs, the survivors continued to experience substantial socio-economic hardships. That their children, traumatized by the Delhi massacres, were unable to concentrate on their lessons which were held in relief camps. That many of them were forced to move away from their old neighbourhoods and schools, and

Introduction

many more had no choice but to start working to support their families right away. The uncomfortable truth is that a majority of the survivors still feel as though their lives have been devastated.

With this book, for the first time ever, the voices and memories of Sikh women have been used to reconstruct—openly and with graphic, often horrifying, detail—not just the Sikh massacre, but also the turbulent politics of the period and the hellish limbo that came in the aftermath of the violence.

From the rise of a political movement, its radical evolution into militancy to the gut-wrenching tragedy of attack on the highest and temporal seat of Sikhs, to Operation Blue Star in 1984 leaving a trail of heartbreak and anguish, and the subsequent chaos and suffering inflicted upon the state due to severe human rights violations—this book will sweep across a region in disarray, and use oral history to build a new narrative of memory that is more inclusive and sensitive to those who were omitted out of the dominant discourse. These are the personal stories of the women of 1984, told for the first time with great courage and honesty.

They must be heard.

1
Saka Neela Tara— Operation Blue Star

Ganji is a small village of about fifty people, where everyone knows everyone else. It is located nine kilometres from the international border between India and Pakistan, close to Narowal which stretches to the Kartarpur corridor at Dera Baba Nanak.

To get there, we took the first left on the inner route to Dorangla, about a kilometre after the Gurdaspur Central Jail on Zaffapur Road. Twelve kilometres down that single, broken road, with a tractor chugging right behind our car, its speakers playing traditional Punjabi pop music that shattered the serenity of the wind-swept paddy fields stretching out on both sides of the car, we turned left again onto a gravelly road that took us straight into Ganji and back into the past to 1984, when time stopped here.

That summer evening in May 1984, when the police arrived in Ganji, it was the first time that the residents of this nondescript village had ever seen so many uniformed men. That same evening, friends became strangers. Relatives ceased visiting each other. Some people turned into informants for the police whilst others were too scared to talk. Police patrolling became a frequent everyday sight—happening mostly twice a day and sometimes more than that. A Maruti Gypsy jeep was permanently stationed at the entrance of the village, a reminder of the constant surveillance the villagers were under. Subsequently, regular raids pushed the village into radio silence, with its menfolk either getting arrested or disappearing altogether from most households.

Rajbir Kaur, a gaunt woman, lived with her two daughters, aged eight and five, and her old mother-in-law in a house at the end of a congested lane. Her husband, Jasbir, had gone missing a few months ago. Jasbir had been a long-time supporter of Harchand Singh Longowal, the patient, grey-bearded president of the Akali Dal,[1] one of the regional political parties of Punjab. Longowal was a popular leader in the state, and his followers formed an influential clique called the Longowal Camp. Since Jasbir's disappearance, Rajbir's mother-in-law had been taking care of the children and managing the household with a meagre income. Rajbir would sit in her open kitchen for hours, brooding and often murmuring to herself. With the passage of time since her last conversation with her husband, her worry for his safety and wellbeing only kept mounting.

Rajbir's travails had started when a cow was butchered in the village and her husband got arrested for it. Later, however, he was let off. A few weeks from then, Rajbir heard that the police were again inquiring about him from their neighbours in the village. Eventually, the police arrived at her doorstep, standing there for hours to intimidate her family. Jasbir did not return home and Rajbir later learnt from her husband's friends that he had once again been arrested by the police, supposedly due to his political affiliations. A sense of uncertainty gnawed at her, compounding the weariness from the persistent harassment. Driven by a steadfast determination to uncover the truth about her husband, she resolved to journey to Amritsar and engage with the party leadership directly. Rajbir took her children and boarded a bus to Amritsar along with her brother. She reached Amritsar on the morning of 31 May 1984.

'Beta, I was terrified,' Rajbir said to me, supporting herself on a pillow and leaning forward. It was the winter of 2019 and I was sitting next to Rajbir in her home in Ganji. Earlier that afternoon, I had walked through the quiet village and seen the scars left behind by its difficult history. There were very few people still living in the village, most of them having left for a better life abroad, and the majority of the houses were locked with big iron locks on the main gates.

'Amritsar was like a garrison town. There were policemen all over the city,' Rajbir continued. 'Men were being separated from women at the bus stand and getting frisked. All of our belongings were thoroughly screened and even the kids were searched.'

The family took a cycle rickshaw from the bus stand to the Golden Temple complex. Because her daughters were famished, Rajbir took them straight to the Guru Ramdas Langar building (community kitchen) of the Golden Temple, where she coincidentally encountered a friend of her husband. When he inquired about the purpose of her visit, she narrated her entire ordeal, from the police harassing her constantly to her search for Jasbir. The man then told her to wait at the Guru Nanak Niwas, a rest house situated across the road from the Langar Hall, and left promising Rajbir that he would look for her husband.

'I was sitting in the lobby of the Guru Nanak Niwas and I could see many people talking loudly and flaunting the names of the groups they belonged to—my husband was a supporter of Harchand Singh Longowal. They were discussing their future plans and talking about such things as fortifications and different strategic positions within the Golden Temple complex. Some people were patiently listening to all of this. The Guru Nanak Niwas was almost full and the number of devotees trickling in was increasing every few hours.'

Things had been eventful within the Golden Temple complex, with a constant stream of youngsters coming and going. Rajbir added that there were all sorts of people in the temple complex; some of them were part of militant outfits but most were innocent pilgrims who had come to observe the anniversary of Guru Arjan Dev's martyrdom, which was to be commemorated two days later on 3 June.

That first evening in Amritsar, Rajbir sat in a corner of the Guru Nanak Niwas with her daughters, waiting for her husband's friend, but he never returned. Eventually, she unfolded a bedsheet and spread it out on the ground for her daughters to sleep on, but she couldn't rest for a single minute. She was worried because she had no money with her. Not only could she not buy any milk for her daughters, she couldn't purchase tickets for their return either.

Hours later, in the dead of night, with light from the main entrance of the sarai penetrating the darkness all around, Rajbir saw someone walking towards her. She immediately recognized that face—it was her husband.

On seeing Jasbir after so many months of constant fear and anxiety, Rajbir was unable to hold back her tears and broke down in front of him. She told him about everything that had happened since he'd left home. Jasbir was silent; he kissed both his daughters' foreheads and then picked them up in his arms. He took his family to the Teja Singh Samundari Hall which was located a block away from the Guru Nanak Niwas. It was the headquarters of the Shiromani Gurdwara Parbandhak Committee, also known as SGPC, which looked after the affairs of all gurdwaras. Most Akali Dal supporters and workers were camping there for the night.

At Teja Singh Samundari Hall, Jasbir told Rajbir that he couldn't stay there with them as he had been assigned political duties by the Akali Dal leadership. He promised, however, that he would come in from time to time to see them. Before leaving, he gave Rajbir some money to buy milk for their daughters. Rajbir was relieved that they were finally together and she wouldn't have to worry about the police raids for the time being.

Much earlier in the day, the charismatic Sikh leader Sant Jarnail Singh Bhindranwale had performed his morning prayers dressed in the traditional long, loose kurta and saffron turban with a kamarkasa (sash) around his waist, carrying two arrows which he always had on him, and then moved to the Guru Ramdas Langar building to address an audience.

On 19 July 1982, Bhai Amrik Singh, the son of late Sant Kartar Singh, and president of the All India Sikh Student Federation, was arrested by the police. This action deeply angered Sant Bhindranwale and he relocated from Mehta Chowk to Guru Nanak Niwas within the Golden Temple Complex. On 20 July, Sant called for a Panthic convention, during which he announced the initiation of a campaign for the release of his associates. Concurrently, the Shiromani Akali Dal had been leading a campaign since April 1982 against the construction of the Satluj-Yamuna Link (SYL) canal.

Meanwhile, Harchand Singh Longowal was inside his headquarters at Teja Singh Samundari Hall. With him were some of his sevadars, party members including the former member of Parliament Balwant Singh Ramoowalia and Manjeet Singh Taran Tarani, his press secretary, and other members of the kitchen cabinet.

Manjeet Singh Taran Tarani, a rare degree-holder in the Longowal camp, was in his early forties at the time. He'd been appointed as the press secretary of Akali Dal because of his educational background. He was well known for his sharp drafting and oratory skills. When I met Manjeet Singh Taran Tarani in Tarn Taran, his hometown, he was a much mellowed man in his seventies. He was wearing a white kurta-pyjama with the Akali blue turban, and had a long flowing white beard. Manjeet Singh vividly recalled everything that had transpired on 1 June 1984. That afternoon, the Longowal camp was discussing the next phase of their agitation: restricting the movement of foodgrains beyond the borders of Punjab. In the early 1980s, the Akalis were protesting and demanding the implementation of the Anandpur Sahib Resolution,[2] which was a charter of political, religious, economic and social demands that they had made on behalf of the Sikh community. Manjeet Singh said that at that point in time, what the Akali movement needed was a strong momentum, and thus it was decided at the meeting to issue a press release stating that there would be no movement of foodgrains outside Punjab.

At 12.45 p.m., while the president of the Akali Dal was still in discussion with his team, sudden gunshots were heard outside. It turned out to be unprovoked firing from the security personnel of the Border Security Force (BSF) and Central Reserve Police Force (CRPF) stationed outside the complex on the orders from the army. The firing was responded to with retaliation from inside. This was the beginning of the catastrophe.

Rajbir and her daughters were in one of the rooms at Teja Singh Samundari Hall when she heard the gunshots. Scared, she held her daughters close and retreated to a corner with other frightened pilgrims.

The volley of shots lasted for about seven hours and left the walls of the Golden Temple complex riddled with bullet holes. Manjeet Singh recalled seeing bullet holes in the walls of the Langar Hall where Sant Jarnail Singh Bhindranwale had held his usual morning congregation and in the windowpanes of Longowal's office as well. He said that this initial round of firing by the security personnel had essentially been meant to check the positions of the militants inside the Golden Temple complex, but there had been no forewarning of the attack. Neither the BSF nor the CRPF had locked down the area beforehand. Unaware of the firing, devotees still poured into the complex, some with children and others with old parents.

Another eyewitness was Kulbir Kaur, a tall and stout girl pursuing a master's degree in English from Hoshiarpur Degree

College at that time. She and some family members had come to the Golden Temple in a trolley attached to a tractor, to offer the year's first harvest of watermelons and wheat from their fields to the community kitchen at the temple. This was a popular tradition followed by Sikh families.

'We reached the Golden Temple complex at around 12.30 p.m., and I remember that at 12.45 p.m., the first bullet was shot just as we entered the Guru Nanak Niwas. All of us panicked. My sister, her children and her husband were also accompanying us, and she was pregnant at the time.'

Kulbir's brother-in-law, Kanwar Dhami, was a bank officer from an influential family of doctors and rare degree holders in Punjab. He was also the leader of the Akal Federation[3] and part of the Akhand Kirtani Jatha.[4] Dhami was in charge of publicity for the Morcha. He was aware of what was going on at the Golden Temple, but he did not tell his wife or his sister-in-law.

Kulbir said that when she entered the Golden Temple complex, she saw men dressed in uniform almost everywhere. The expansive Golden Temple complex houses revered structures, including Harmandir Sahib, Akal Takht Sahib, Holy Sarovar along with the Ramgarhia Bunga, the eighteenth-century, three-storey redstone watch towers. A significant feature of the Temple is the Guru's Langar, one of the world's largest community kitchens. A road divides the Temple and hostel complexes, with the residential area housing structures such as the Teja Singh Samundri Hall, Guru Nanak Niwas, Guru Ram Das Sarai and other buildings. The Temple complex serves as a vibrant representation of Sikh heritage. Kulbir Kaur thought it was normal that the army would patrol their village during the harvest season, but she was surprised to see security personnel within the Temple complex. Hours after the firing incident, when things seemed to have quietened down a little, Kulbir and her cousins decided to visit the Harmandir Sahib despite the shots they had heard. Kulbir described the atmosphere at the Golden Temple as tense, with gunshots echoing every five minutes from outside, met with sporadic gunfire from inside, as militants engaged primarily from the Langar Hall building. It was during their parikrama (circumambulation) of the temple that Kulbir saw a baby feeder covered in blood lying on the ground. Even now, decades later, when she closes her eyes, Kulbir says that she can still vividly recall the sight.

Immediately after the firing incident, Sant Longowal summoned all the Akali leaders for an emergency meeting on 2 June. The press secretaries—Manjeet Singh Taran Tarani and Balwant Singh Ramoowalia—started contacting the Akali leadership, members of Parliament, legislators and others, summoning them all to the SGPC office the next day.

Press secretary Manjeet Singh recalls that telephone calls were made to Gurcharan Singh Tohra, president of the SGPC in Patiala and Prakash Singh Majitha, Akali leader at his village, Majitha. Prakash Singh Badal was also contacted, but he couldn't attend the meeting because he was in his home in Terai, Uttar Pradesh. Surjit Singh Barnala was in Chandigarh, and another important leader, Balwant Singh, was abroad. To make sure that all the leaders attended this urgent meeting, telegrams were sent to each of them separately.

The firing incident had infuriated the otherwise calm Harchand Singh Longowal. In the press statement he issued afterwards, he said:

By opening fire on the Golden Temple, the government has begun a new fight with the Sikh quom. With this, the governments facade of secularism has been unveiled. Every bullet on Golden Temple has pierced through the heart of every Sikh. I appeal to Sants of Sikh religion, the do and die squad, followers of Guru Nanak, that the Sikh community has been plunged into a new crisis and at this hour of trial, they should be prepared for the supreme sacrifice.[5]

Longowal also made every effort possible to establish contact with the President of India, Giani Zail Singh, on the telephone and speak to him about what had happened. However, Zail Singh did not answer his calls. Manjeet Singh said that when Longowal finally managed to speak to the President, Zail Singh told him that he was helpless.

Gurcharan Singh Tohra repeated the sentiments of Jathedar[6] Longowal and said:

The attack on Golden Temple is an open challenge to the Sikh community. After the Mughals, only the present government has challenged the self-respect of the Sikh Community. Behind the garb of secularism, there is a blatant display of communalism. The religious places of minorities are not safe in this country. By attacking the Golden Temple the government has caused deep wounds in the hearts of the Sikhs. If there is slightest self-esteem and dignity among the Sikh Congress MPs and legislators they must resign from the party.[7]

He also wrote to the prime minister and expressed his anguish over the monstrous attack on the Golden Temple:

> It is with a sense of extreme pain and regret that I wish to draw your attention to the most brutal, most savage and most monstrous manner in which a relentless and senseless campaign of repression and oppression has been going on against the Sikhs for the last two years. The Sikh leadership has been exercising utmost restraint in the hope that the government may see the path of reason and may ultimately relent. However, the mounting fury frustrated our hopes. The climax of this ruthless and callous campaign was reached yesterday when the CRPF and BSF, obviously on the orders of the government, launched a seven hours savage and shameless attack on the Holy Golden Temple, killing a dozen of pilgrims and grievously injuring three dozen more. Never since Ahmad Shah Abdali, from whose clutches thousands of Hindu girls were saved by the Sikhs once, was this holiest shrine attacked, not even during the alien British rule. I wonder if the perpetrators of these wounds on the fair face of the Holy Golden Temple and in the heart of every Sikh, do really realize that these wounds may well bleed the entire country white ultimately. I would sincerely request you to contain this fire before it assumes a form of conflagration which may engulf the entire country.[8]

As the sun dipped below the horizon that evening, a significant turn of events unfolded. The Jathedar of Akal Takht, Kirpal Singh, and the revered head priest of the Golden Temple, Giani Sahib Singh, came together to issue a joint statement, expressing their condemnation of the incident:

> Since long the Indian Government was planning to destroy the cultural identity of the Sikhs—Darbar Sahib, Shri Harmandir Sahib. To execute the sinister plan, the CRPF has attacked the sacred shrine on June 1, 1984 with artillery fire. The unprovoked artillery attack in which dozen Sikh pilgrims were killed and the sacred shrine recived bullet injuries, was the last murderous attack on the cultural and religious identies of Sikhs. All the organizations of Sikhs present within Golden Temple complex remained united and set a living example of steadfast confidence and rising spirit (Chardi Kala) of the Khalsa. Keeping in view the unprovoked attack on the the Golden Temmple, we appeal to all the organizations of the Khalsa Panth to defeat the sinister designs of demoniac forces and repulse the attack of the CRPF and BSF. To uphold the sanctity of Sri Durbar Sahib, Golden Temple.[9]

The government's response was to clamp down on Amritsar with a thirty two-hour curfew till 3 June 1984. In fact, by late afternoon on 1 June, the Golden Temple had been encircled by the Bihar Regiment of the Indian Army. Major General Kuldip Singh Brar, the clean-shaven Jat-Sikh commander of 9 Division, was commissioned to spearhead the operation against the Sikh millitants who were trained by the decorated soldier-turned-renegade Shabeg Singh, a former major general. Major General

Shabeg Singh had trained the Mukti Bahini guerrillas in their fight to liberate East Pakistan, now known as Bangladesh, in 1971.

General Arun Shridhar Vaidya was the chief of the Indian Army in 1984. Assisted by Lt General Krishnaswamy Sundarji as General Officer Commanding-in-Chief Western Command, he planned and coordinated the entire operation. Major General Brar had command of the action and was operating under Lt General Sundarji's supervision.

On the night of 2 June 1984, in an unscheduled broadcast on All India Radio and Doordarshan, Indira Gandhi appealed to all Akali leaders to call off their agitation and accept the peaceful settlement proposed by the government. She said, 'I appeal to Akali leaders to call off their threatened agitation and accept the peaceful settlement which we have offered.'[10] The prime minister ended her address to the nation with the words, 'To all sections of Punjabis, I appeal, do not shed blood, shed hatred.'[11]

But the spilling of blood was already written. Soon after her speech, another message was broadcast by All India Radio and Doordarshan, announcing that the army had been called into Punjab to aid civil authorities. It was the first time in the history of independent India that the complete control of security and state was given to the army. There was also a high deployment of BSF and CRPF personnel in and around the Golden Temple complex. From the speech that Gandhi gave on 2 June and from the developments that followed, it was clear that an attack was inevitable.

The 9th Infantry Division stationed in Meerut was deployed to Amritsar for the primary assault. Brigadier D.V. Rao, leading the 350 Infantry Brigade, received orders to initiate an operation within the Golden Temple and to coordinate reconnaissance efforts within the compound. The 10 Guards, 26 Madras, 12 Bihar and 9 Kumaon infantry regiments of the Indian Army were mobilized for the operation.

In the heart of Amritsar, a swift and ominous transformation took place. As night descended on 3 June, all telephone connections in the city and at the sacred complex were abruptly severed. A haunting silence enveloped the Akalis, who, if inclined, found themselves unable to reach out to the government or the army to avert the impending tragedy that awaited innocent pilgrims. Against this backdrop, the curtains lifted on the sombre initiation of Operation Blue Star.

These subsequent events raised some obvious questions. If Indira Gandhi's appeal for peace was indeed a profound expression of concern, why then did the government give full control to the army immediately after the peace settlement proposal was put on the table?

Operation Blue Star cast a heavy shadow on the hearts of many Sikhs who deeply believed in the principles of the Constitution and dedicated service to their country. Among these individuals was Simranjit Singh Mann, whose father was a former speaker of Punjab Vidhan Sabha.

In 2014, I met Simranjit Singh Mann, the president of the Sikh political party Shiromani Akali Dal Amritsar at his palatial Fatehgarh Sahib residence. Mann is a very calm, well-spoken former police officer and a three-term member of Parliament. He resigned from his post as group commandant of the Central Industrial Security Force (CISF) in Bombay to protest against Operation Blue Star and the subsequent anti-Sikh violence of 1984.

When I arrived at his home, a member of his domestic staff first escorted me to a drawing room which had silver artefacts in every corner and a vividly patterned Chesterfield sofa. Then, about fifteen minutes later, I was ushered into a dining room where Mann served me breakfast at a ten-seater dining table. We discussed geopolitics and Punjab as we ate. 'Tell me, Sanam, where in the world does the head of a country take the help of foreign nations to attack his or her own people? Mrs Gandhi did this, and her friends in England and Soviet helped her,' said Mann.

We were talking about how after initially refusing to send the army into the Golden Temple complex, Indira Gandhi eventually discussed different attack options, including sending in commandos inside the complex. According to a letter from Margaret Thatcher's principal private secretary, dated 6 February 1984, Indira Gandhi had sought advice from the British government and the elite Special Air Services (SAS) in the early months of 1984 about the situation in Punjab.[12]

Thatcher, it seems, had agreed to help her Indian counterpart because she wanted to increase the sale of British defence equipment to India.[13] The British government even sent an officer from the SAS unit, which is known for covert reconnaissance, counterterrorism, direct action and hostage rescue, to India.

The SAS officer visited the Golden Temple on Gandhi's and Rameshwar Nath Kao's, her de-facto national security adviser's, request. Kao was born into a Kashmiri Pandit family in Benaras; his family migrated from Srinagar district of Jammu and Kashmir. He was India's spymaster and the founding head of the Research and Analysis Wing (R&AW). He was also the key advisor on Punjab.

It was the British SAS officer who drew up a plan to kidnap Sant Jarnail Singh Bhindranwale.[14] This plan was named Operation Sundown, and preparations for it began at the Sarsawa army base in Uttar Pradesh. Disguised as pilgrims, operatives from the Special Group (SG) visited the Golden Temple complex to study its layout. A seamless plan involving two transport helicopters and a ground assault team was then devised, and a two-storeyed model of Guru Nanak Niwas was made out of hessian cloth for training purposes. For weeks the SG commandos practiced hard, but fearing high casualties, Gandhi later dismissed Operation Sundown.

However, just two months later, she gave the green signal for the bloodiest operation against her own people which also ushered in an era of homegrown militancy in Punjab. Till date, no one knows who actually ordered Operation Blue Star and there is no record of whether the decision was an oral order or a written one.

In the early 1980s, Amritsar was a city on the brink of war with a political crisis unfolding in Punjab and a multitude of power claimants locked in an aggressive tug-of-war. Unwilling to abandon their popularity, even typically moderate leaders such as the Akalis shifted away from their moderate stance when the government showed reluctance to address the Punjab issue. Faced with the fear of their position weakening and aiming to salvage their influence among Sikhs, they embraced agitation. The Rasta Roko Morcha, a road blockage protest, was initiated by the Akali Dal in April 1983 under the leadership of Harchand Singh Longowal.

Amid clashes with the police during the 'rasta roko' agitation, the otherwise calm Longowal, the Morcha's leader, issued an ultimatum, expressing impatience and warning Prime Minister Indira Gandhi against playing with fire. Longowal declared the formation of a volunteer corps named Sirjiware—a do-or-die suicide squad comprising a hundred thousand Sikhs from Punjab's 12,500 villages to intensify the protest.

Punjab fell into chaos due to the tumultuous interplay of political forces, primarily driven by Prime Minister Indira Gandhi's intrusive policies. Through the years, the political stronghold of the Congress had been diminishing, posing a threat to the dominance of the party in upcoming parliamentary elections. In response, she identified the steadfast Akalis as convenient targets to incite a Hindu backlash. This is evident from Gandhi's withdrawal on three occasions from a previously negotiated settlement with the protesting Akalis. Internal rifts within the ranks of Congress leaders, exemplified by figures like Giani Zail Singh and Darbara Singh, became pronounced. Their ongoing manoeuvres, conflicts and the communalized environment they contributed to began to jeopardize the very social fabric of the state. Simultaneously, factionalism deepened among Akali leaders, intensifying the storm that swept the once-serene land. Punjab then echoed with the complexities of a story spun by political ambitions and internal strife.

In the months of April and May 1984, the jails in Punjab were filled with people who had courted arrest during the Dharam Yudh Morcha, meaning 'righteous campaign', a religious and political movement initiated in Punjab on 4 August 1982. Led by the Akali Dal in collaboration with Sant Jarnail Singh Bhindranwale, its primary goal was to achieve a set of devolutionary objectives outlined in the Anandpur Sahib Resolution. Dharam Yudh became the clarion call for many young people. Jasmeet Kaur, a diminutive young college student at that time, was encouraged by her father to court arrest for the same cause.

Jasmeet's father was an inspector with the Crime Investigation Department (CID). His job was to gather information about what was going on within the Golden Temple and record Sant Bhindranwale's speeches at the daily public audience held in the terrace of the Langar Hall. Every morning he would leave home with his audio recorder, an imported set, wrapped up in a crisp white handkerchief. He would make his way to the Langar Hall and sit in the front row, close to Sant Bhindranwale to record every single detail of his speech.

After listening to Sant Bhindranwale for months, Jasmeet's father had a change of heart and became his follower. He would return home in the evening every day and tell his family about the things he had heard in the day at the daily public audience. He encouraged them to listen to Bhindranwale's speeches as well. But in spite of being a devout Sikh man, Jasmeet's father was duty-bound too. Every night, therefore, he would sit alone at his desk and type up a daily report to send to his high command.

When I asked Jasmeet about how she got involved with the Dharam Yudh Morcha, she replied, 'My father said it's the duty of every Sikh to support the Dharam Yudh Morcha and Sant Jarnail Singh Bhindranwale, and that we must not sit at home but be there at the Golden Temple. That's when everybody in the family—my grandparents, mother and siblings—started to come out and court arrest.'

During the Dharam Yudh Morcha, hundreds of people courted arrest and these numbers increased dramatically from hundreds to thousands as the movement gained momentum among the young people across Punjab. Sikh youth from other Indian states also came to Punjab to show their solidarity. In the beginning, even the Punjab police was very supportive and respectful towards the movement, probably because there was a widespread discontent among Sikhs regarding political and religious issues.

'In the afternoon, Sant Jarnail Singh Bhindranwale used to flag off the first batch of people to court arrest and all of us would then walk to the kotwali (police station) in Amritsar,' said Jasmeet Kaur as she recalled the events of 1984. 'At the kotwali, which was located close to Jallianwala Bagh,[15] there used to be langar for everyone and from there, at about 5 p.m., the police would take us to Ludhiana jail.'

Jasmeet's father was also posted at the kotwali in Amritsar, but he had instructed his family to not speak to him while they were there, saying that no one should know they were related. That could have jeopardized his position and job.

Once in the Ludhiana jail, the police mostly detained those arrested for a few hours before releasing all of them. Very rarely were people kept overnight in the jails, for fear of overcrowding. Sometimes, the detainees were given ten rupees each to take the Shan-e-Punjab train back to Amritsar and at times, police vehicles even dropped them to the railway station.

Jasmeet said that for a few weeks she was in the Ludhiana jail almost every day. She made friends with other Sikh families who came every day to court arrest. On days when no one from her family came along with her, Jasmeet went with her newfound friends. On 31 May 1984, Jasmeet returned home to Ajnala on her father's request after she fell ill.

By 1984, Punjab was tense. An eerie sense of doom hovered over the state, especially the city of Amritsar. Many innocent people were targeted and killed by both militants and state actors. It was complete chaos and Punjab was pushed to the brink of crisis by political leaders for their personal gains; all those at the helm of affairs belonged to the Congress Party.

Manjeet Singh Taran Tarani told me that with the army determined to attack the Golden Temple, the only option left was to convince Sant Jarnail Singh Bhindranwale to come out and surrender.

Therefore, on 2 June Jathedar Gurcharan Singh Tohra, the only Akali Dal member who was on good terms with Sant Jarnail Singh Bhindranwale, thought that he could convince the latter to come out of the Golden Temple complex. He crossed the road from the hostel complex[16] and walked through the Langar Hall and the Manji Sahib Gurdwara where terrified pilgrims were huddled together in small groups. Tohra entered the Golden Temple and found sandbags covering the gates and arches where armed young Sikhs had taken up their defensive positions.

When Tohra met Sant Bhindranwale, the former tried to convince him that resistance was going to be futile because the army was resolute in its mission to capture them. But Sant Bhindranwale rebuked Tohra, calling him and Longowal representatives of Indira Gandhi for talking about surrendering to her.

Manjeet Singh also pointed out that when Tohra had stepped out of the hostel complex, the firing from outside and inside had suddenly stopped and it did not resume until he came back inside. He added, 'Tohra wasn't one who would risk himself unless he had some surety.'

By the night of 2 June 1984, Punjab was cut off from the rest of the world. All the phone lines were snapped; rail, bus and air services were stopped; and the international border from Kashmir to Ganganagar was sealed. The press was gagged as well: all foreign journalists and those from national dailies were asked to leave Punjab immediately. Those who did not obey the order were picked up by paramilitary and police personnel and dropped off at Ambala city, Haryana. No one knew what was happening in Amritsar.

The meeting that had been called by the president of Akali Dal, Harchand Singh Longowal, after the firing incident of 1 June did not happen on the scheduled date because Gurucharan Singh Tohra, Sukhdev Singh Dhindsa (former MLA and Rajya Sabha member) and Balwinder Singh were the only ones who managed to reach the Golden Temple. The meeting was then postponed to 4 June 1984.

Meanwhile, within the Temple complex, Sant Bhindranwale instructed those of his men who did not wish to stay to leave. The wives of the followers were also encouraged to depart.

Simultaneously, numerous pilgrims who were present inside the sarais chose to leave through Bagwali Gali, a lane behind the hostel complex, when the army temporarily relaxed the curfew on 3 June. As these individuals exited the temple complex, many were barefoot—a clear indicator that they had been inside the Golden Temple. Given the army's scrutiny of individuals without shoes, locals assisted many of these men with a change of clothes and a pair of shoes.

That same day, on 3 June, Sant Jarnail Singh Bhindranwale's right-hand man, Amrik Singh, son of former Damdami Taksal[17] chief Sant Kartar Singh, came to his room near the Langar Hall building to meet his mother, wife and daughters. With him were six or seven men armed with guns slung across their shoulders and rounds of bullets hanging around their waists.

Inside the room, Amrik Singh said to his wife, Satwant Kaur, 'It's now your responsibility to see that our daughters get the best education.' One of his daughters would later recall this in an interview with Sangat TV in 2012.

Harmeet Kaur, his wife replied, 'But where are you going? You will be here to guide them, right?'

'Our time has come,' Amrik Singh said. 'We have been waiting for this day forever. We will soon be martyred, but you don't have to worry. God will be there to guide you.'

His daughter, who was six years old at that time, recalls holding the corner of her father's robe and refusing to leave Amritsar without him. Harmeet Kaur, pregnant at that time, also refused to leave the city without her husband and insisted on staying within the temple complex with her younger daughter. Witnessing this, Amrik Singh asked his mother to take his elder daughter and leave Amritsar before the curfew was imposed again. He said that somebody would escort them safely to the bus stand because anything could happen in Amritsar.

Amrik Singh did not try to convince his wife to leave the Golden Temple complex. Instead, he said to her, 'All right, then pray that their bullets only hit me in my chest.' However, he made it very clear that he wouldn't stay with them; he had to go back to fight. But before leaving, he told Harmeet Kaur to go and sit where the other women and children within the temple complex were sheltered.

The next day, around evening, some women and children, mostly from pilgrim families still caught inside the Golden Temple complex, gathered in the Langar Hall in search of safety and food. However, amidst all the incessant firing, food had not been cooked. When Amrik Singh got to know about this, he sent his brother-in-law with some bread and water for his pregnant wife and for the others in the Langar Hall.

Harmeet Kaur was elated on seeing her brother. When she enquired about her husband, he told her, 'He is with Sant Jarnail Singh Bhindranwale, and they are fine.' She tried to stop him from leaving the Langar Hall because they could hear the gunfight going on outside, but he refused to stay back, saying, 'My brothers are waiting for me. They need me.'

Harmeet's brother deputed Giani Puran Singh, Granthi,[18] in Harmandir Sahib to safely take all the women and children out of the Langar Hall building to his residential quarter. Giani Puran Singh's residence was located on Shaheed Bunga Lane, with a discreet door opening into the parikarama zone. The army was unaware of both the door and the lane.

That very night, Giani Puran Singh and some others decided to try and leave the Langar Hall building and make their way to Singh's residential quarters. A group of Sikh men and women, accompanied by Giani Puran Singh, courageously exited the Langar Hall amid a relentless hail of bullets. Women hid behind the marble pillars of the colonnaded Parikrama around the Golden Temple in order to safely cross over without coming in the way of the firing.

Despite Harmeet's deliberate and cautious steps, compelled by her pregnancy, with unwavering determination, she pressed on and reached the revered Akal Takht. However, the continuous gunfire enveloping her made each subsequent move a challenge. Amid this tumult, a compassionate young Sikh man gallantly carried her younger daughter.

She was now near the main door of the Golden Temple, which was right in front of the Akal Takht Sahib. This was an entirely open space and it was also the centre of the main assault, making Harmeet and all the other women there clear and easy targets. It seemed to be an impossible situation—they could neither go forward nor retreat back. Somehow though, in the middle of a rather heavy exchange of bullets, Harmeet managed to take a few steps back and find refuge behind a pillar.

As she stood there in sheer fright, Harmeet spotted her husband and some other Sikh men standing at one of the windows near the Akal Takht Sahib and waving his hands at her. However, she was uncertain about what he wanted to convey to her. Was he beckoning her to leave? Or perhaps he was telling her to stay hidden. Ultimately though, after much delay, Harmeet was finally able to make it to the hidden door with the help of Giani Puran Singh.[19]

In the early hours of 4 June, the firing was intensified yet again and power supply to the Golden Temple complex was cut off. This further complicated matters for those inside the Temple complex as they were already facing an acute shortage of water and food.

The intense gunfight of 4 June had brought morning prayers to a halt within the Temple complex, and Gurucharan Singh Tohra along with Sahib Singh, the chief priest, had agreed to not begin recitals from the Holy Book from many places in the complex. The gunfight had also caused a lot of damage to tall structures within the Temple complex, like the elevated water tank and the Ramgarhia Bunga. Within five minutes of coming under heavy firing, the sandbag fortifications that had been built around the Bunga had been reduced to dust.[20]

Rachpal Singh, Sant Bhindranwale's scholarly looking bespectacled secretary, was taking a bath when the morning attack occurred. His wife, Pritam Kaur, was outside her room in the Golden Temple complex with their eighteen-day-old son. She rushed back inside the room when the firing started and asked her husband why he hadn't told her about the attack.

He replied, 'Now you know it. When we are here to attain martyrdom, why to think?' He then asked Pritam Kaur to leave their first-floor room and shift to the ground floor.[21]

According to Manjeet Singh, on 5 June at around 8 a.m., the first bullet had hit Harchand Singh Longowal's room which had remained safe until then. Abinashi Singh, who was the assistant to the president of the SGPC, suggested that Sant Longowal move to Tohra's room. He said that both the presidents should be together at this crucial time. Balwant Singh Ramoowalia, Dara Singh, Manjeet Singh Taran Tarani and other members of Longowal's kitchen cabinet including a few sevadars went to Jathedar Tohra's room on the ground floor of Ramdas Sarai for safety.

That same day, some time in the afternoon, around 120 people, including some children, came out of the Golden Temple with their hands held up above their heads. They were immediately taken into police custody and moved to the city's kotwali.

Meanwhile, at around 9.30 a.m. that morning, Pritam's husband went to the Akal Takht Sahib to meet Sant Jarnail Singh Bhindranwale and asked him what their next step was going to be. The sant replied, 'Tell everyone to hold their positions till their last breath; this is our last command.'

Two hours later, as the assault intensified and Pritam Kaur's husband told her that they could be martyred anytime now, she asked him to recite the *Kirtan Sohila* (nighttime prayers) while she fed their son.

Rachpal Singh said to his wife, '*Boleya chaleya maaf karin*. If I have ever done or said anything wrong, forgive me.' Pritam Kaur remained silent, emotionally overwhelmed by the realization that these could be her husband's last words to her. She touched her husband's feet and replied, 'You have been very kind, please forgive me if I have ever said anything unkind.' Rachpal Singh simply kissed his son's forehead and the couple exchanged their last fateh (the Sikh salutation, 'Waheguru Ji ka Khalsa, Waheguru Ji ki Fateh').

Reminiscing about that time, Pritam Kaur was able to recount every second of that day. She said, 'A flash of light would come in from the space below the doors and blind us for a few seconds, followed by the deafening sounds of bombs. I could hear the sound of tank treads moving outside our room, proceeding towards the Akal Takht.'[22]

Hours later, at around 12.15 a.m. on 6 June, a single bullet suddenly tore through the air and pierced her baby's back before hitting Pritam Kaur in her chest. The child died on the spot, while Pritam fell to the ground. Even as Rachpal Singh bent over to help his wife and son, another bullet struck him in the head and he succumbed to his injuries almost instantaneously. Pritam lay in a growing pool of blood but remained alive, lying in pain, her dead son on her chest and her dead husband next to her.

Of that day, Manjeet Singh recalled, 'Bullets were raining down on us unremittingly. We were sitting in one corner of Sant Longowal's room, worried for the safety of Sant Longowal. Suddenly, about four or five young men with guns on their shoulders entered the room. They had a metallic box, possibly a radio transmitter, with them. They pointed their guns at us and told us that the box was connected with General Zia-ul-Haq in Pakistan. They instructed Jathedar Tohra and Sant Longowal to declare the formation of Khalistan so that the Pakistani Army could launch an attack against Indian forces. The jathedars, however, kept quiet. After a few tense seconds, Tohra told them that this was a matter that had to be decided between Sant Jarnail Singh Bhindranwale and Indira Gandhi since it was the former who was leading the movement. It would only be fair to ask Sant Bhindranwale to declare the creation of Khalistan. On hearing Tohra's response, the youth left the room as suddenly as they had appeared and never came back.'

Manjeet Singh said that he had never seen those young men before. He was not even sure whether they were actually Sikh militants or if they were government agents who had infiltrated the Golden Temple to extract a declaration of the formation of Khalistan and thereby provide the government with a justification to attack them.

Outside the Golden Temple complex, things were looking a little bleak. At the complex, General Brar's casualties were rapidly increasing. To ease the pressure on commandoes and the infantry, he sought Lt General Sundarji's approval to employ tanks. General Brar planned to use tanks to breach Akal Takht, but had to wait for clearance from New Delhi. K.P. Singh Deo, the then minister of state for defence, was heading the operations room in Delhi along with former territorial army (second line of defence after the Indian Army) major Arun Singh, who was also a member of the former royal family of Kapurthala. He was also close to

Rajiv Gandhi. Two hours later came the clearance. Six tanks were deployed.

Then at 3.00 a.m. on 6 June, General Brar opted for the disastrous action for which history will never forgive him. First, they called the armoured personnel carriers (APC) to barge into the Akal Takht. The marble staircase at the entrance made it difficult; thus, a tank was called to run down the steps and make way for the APCs to enter. The generals felt that they could neutralize the militants but when the militants fired an anti-tank rocket launcher, an RPG-7 of Chinese origin, they were in for another shock. It perforated the APC and wounded its commander, Captain Jagdev Singh. A Howitzer was used to threaten Sant and his men to surrender but it failed to do its job. Finally, from the Vijayanta tank's main armament, high explosive squash head shells were pounded on Akal Takht Sahib, desecrating it, and significantly damaging the gurdwara complex.

The shelling also significantly damaged buildings in the residential areas around the gurdwara complex, especially in the Atta Mandi locality, which is just a few metres away. Those who stayed in these areas were given ten minutes to vacate their homes. An unknown number of people lost their lives while leaving their homes for a secure location. One of the residents, who wishes to stay anonymous, said, 'We had only ten minutes to leave our home. Scared and not sure of our return, we took what little we could. But my mother didn't come with us. Her parents were refugees. She knew the hardships, and she wanted to carry her cash and gold safely with her. She decided to make her way across the terraces instead. She had done this earlier as well. We all reached my father's elder brother's home safely, but my mother didn't make it. We found cash and gold with her bullet-riddled body on one of the terraces.'

Over 350 bullets riddled the dome of the Golden Temple. One bullet pierced the cushion on which the Shri Guru Granth Sahib was placed, pushing through as many as eighty-two pages of the book itself. Most of the items in the toshakhana[23] were destroyed. The chandani, a canopy presented by the Nizam of Hyderabad, was destroyed. All the handwritten hukamnamas, penned by different Sikh gurus across the ages, were lost as well.

The bodies of Sant Jarnail Singh Bhindranwale, Baba Thara Singh and Bhai Amrik Singh were found inside Akal Takht Sahib. They remained faithful to their commitments and died fighting. They were brought out and cremated. As Punjab was still under a curfew, the roll of white cloth that was required for Sant Jarnail Singh Bhindranwale's cremation was arranged by the wife of an official from the deputy commissioner's office[24] Sub-divisional magistrate S.S. Dhillon was assigned the task of taking the sant's mortal remains for immersion in the Kirtarpur Sahib.

At the Guru Ram Das sarai, Manjeet Singh said that they were all made to sit in lines while the army searched the rooms inside. He was also asked by Colonel Onkar Goraya to prepare a separate list of SGPC staff members, and men, women and children. In the sarai, most people were pilgrims, drawn to honour the martyrdom day of the fifth Guru, Arjan Dev Ji, who found themselves ensnared by the imposed curfew.

'On the top floor of the sarai, there were Sant Jarnail Singh Bhindranwale's supporters who opened fire on the soldiers as they searched the sarai and the army retaliated by firing back, which caused chaos to erupt at the sarai. A young man and his infant son who was maybe about two or three years old were also killed. The mother picked up her son and put him on her dead husband's chest. It's been more than three decades now, but whenever I close my eyes, that scene comes back to me,' said Manjeet Singh.

At around four in the afternoon on 6 June, Sant Longowal, Jathedar Tohra, Bibi Amarjeet Kaur, head of Akhand Kirtani Jatha, and about five others were brought out of the Golden Temple complex in an APC and taken to a state guest house. Jathedar Tohra collapsed inside the APC due to suffocation, but his sevadars helped revive him.

Manjeet Singh continued, 'I don't know how we managed to stay alive without water for two whole days in that dreadful June heat, not to mention the continuous firing. When we arrived at the guest house, we were not only tired but most of us were numb as well. I drank three jugs of water straight, and then we were separated from the jathedars. They were kept in a closed room for seven hours. The next day, they took Jathedar Tohra and Harchand Singh Longowal to some undisclosed location. Later, they took away Bibi Amarjeet Kaur also.'

Manjeet Singh was released the same day, but he was picked up again from his home a week later. He then spent six months at the Nabha Jail in solitary confinement.

Following the conclusion of Operation Blue Star, a brief two-hour reprieve from the curfew was granted on 6 June. During this window, disoriented and infuriated Sikhs hurried to Harmandir Sahib, covering distances of 5–10 kilometres by foot as vehicular traffic was prohibited. Outside the clock tower and Jallianwala Bagh, APC tanks and RCL guns stood sentinel. Despite their anguish, little could be done by the Sikhs who were swiftly turned away. Police were summoned to evacuate casualties from the parikarma area.

The scenes were far from simple for those detained from the Golden Temple complex, as they found themselves under the custody of the army instead of the police. Stripped of any additional clothing, the detainees were left with only what they were wearing. Several teams, each comprising an officer from the Indian Army, CBI, Intelligence Bureau (IB), and the state police's CID, were established for simultaneous processing, conducting interrogations of the detainees held in temporary jails.

Along with her brother and daughters, Rajbir Kaur was hiding in one of the rooms of the Samundri Hall. Her husband Jasbir had managed to escape from the Golden Temple complex through Baghwali Gali on 5 June. Rajbir says she felt relieved when she heard about her husband escaping safely because she thought the army wouldn't stop women and children from leaving the temple complex, and once the firing stopped she could return to Gurdaspur with her daughters.

But after the firing was over, returning home was not as easy as Rajbir had imagined. She recalled how when they came out of their hiding place, they found the terrible smell of blood and fire pervading the entire complex. Rajbir also said that there were so many dead bodies lying on the ground that they could barely walk without stepping on them. She and her daughters, along with the other women and children, were not allowed to leave and were instead detained by the Indian Army.

The Golden Temple was not the only gurdwara to be desecrated that night. The Indian Army surrounded thirty-seven other gurdwaras in Punjab. In Patiala, the army faced much resistance from the Gurdwara Dukhniwaran Sahib. As part of a coordinated combing operation led by Sikh officer Major General Gurdial Singh, a minimum of fifty-six individuals lost their lives. Although the army reported 20 casualties, local Sikhs contested the figure, asserting that the death toll reached 56.[25]

Within the Golden Temple complex, the water in the sarovar (holy tank) had turned yellowish red. The Parikrama area was a gory mosaic of red, olive and blue. The entire complex was strewn with dead bodies. Sweepers described the curdling sight of the blood. When they tried to lift a body by its limbs, flesh simply peeled away from it and came into their hands. They had to rip their turbans and dupattas and tie them around the bodies in order to pick them up and put them on stretchers to be taken to the trucks which would then carry them to Guru Tegh Bahadur Hospital.

Municipality vehicles transported human bodies from the complex for a post mortem; a pure formality manually performed before cremation. Later, several identical details emerged from these post mortem reports: the doctors had recorded multiple instances of male corpses with their hands tied behind their backs. The question that arose then was that if these young Sikhs boys had been killed during an exchange of bullets, why were their hands tied behind their backs?

Rajbir Kaur, along with her daughters, were taken to the local camp set up by the security forces. There were no arrangements, not even water. On the same day more than forty children were detained from the Golden Temple complex. These children's misery didn't finish with their arbitrary detention; they also had to face coercive questioning by two federal agencies, the CBI and the IB. They were detained in Punjab's high-security prisons. Fifteen students of Damdamitaksal had been labelled as dangerous terrorists. These children were not separated from hardcore criminals as the law requires, but were instead kept together.

Rajbir witnessed security personnel beating young boys in the age group of 18–25. She told me that these boys were pilgrims like them, but they were picked up because they were not wearing chappals; some of them were picked up because they were Amrithdhari Sikhs. The security personnel had no understanding that a Sikh pilgrim would generally avoid wearing slippers anywhere in the temple complex. 'We were treated as terrorists, there was no water or the food. Security forces personnel gave us food on the second night, some uncooked lentils and bread. We knew we are in no position to complain. Bathrooms were overflowing, and everything was stinking. And above all, the unbearable heat of June. Even animals are treated better.' She said, in her room there were almost 70 or 80 women and none of them slept that night. The screams of young boys being tortured in the room next to theirs was a living nightmare. That nightmare would continue over the days to come, as one by one, each of them were called for interrogation. 'It was hellish, I overheard one security personnel saying "If these militant women agree, then take them and enjoy with them." They were planning to rape us,' Rajbir said. 'I told all the other ladies and we decided that if anyone tried to touch us then we would jump from the roof along with our kids. Luckily, next day senior officers came and nothing happened. On the third day, we were handed over to Punjab police for further investigations. Officials from the Punjab police helped us with food and water. They used to bring homecooked meals for us. They were kind towards our kids and gave them whatever little they could. But they did not allow our families to meet us. My father came to meet me with food and clothes for the kids. They did not let him see me but they did give me the stuff he had brought for the kids.'

Rajbir and her daughters were eventually shifted to the Gumtala prison for nineteen days. Throughout this period, Rajbir's daughters stayed with her in spite of being unwell for most of the time.

'We were in prison for no fault of ours. We did not have a choice, nor were we ever given any choice or agency to begin with,' said Rajbir.

When Bibi Rajinder Kaur, the daughter of Master Tara Singh, a prominent Sikh religious and political leader, visited Rajbir, she brought some clothes, food and milk with her. A week later, Jasbir's uncle got them all out on bail.

'We came home and thought this is it; now there is no leader, no movement—but we were absolutely naive. It started all over again.'

After coming out of prison, Rajbir didn't stay in one place for over a week. She kept running from one place to the next in order to hide. 'Beta, I almost spent an entire year on the road, walking day and night with my daughters. There was no other way to survive. If you were seen at one place more than once, then the police would come and pick you up. Whenever I visited my relatives during that period, they would try to get rid of us as soon as possible. They would give us something to eat, but no one was willing to let us stay, and they of course had their reasons for it.'

When I met with her, Rajbir didn't blame her family for their behaviour. The times were such, she said. The police would have picked up anyone giving food or shelter to militants or anyone suspected of being a militant. 'Our only fault was that we were present during those unfortunate days.'

Months after Operation Blue Star, she reunited with her husband in Delhi, later moving to Jalandhar and residing in Patiala for a few months before relocating once again. Despite changing locations, the family lived in constant fear, spending two years in hiding, unable to reveal their true identities due to the persistent threat of police harassment, till Surjit Singh Barnala became the chief minister of Punjab. Tragically, Rajbir passed away due to a long-term illness in 2023.

After Operation Blue Star, hundreds of Sikh women witnessed hell coming to life due to the securitization of the state—lonely, overworked and harassed by the army and the police, molested and beaten for failing to produce their men, many of whom were in hiding. Sometimes, over a hundred army personnel would raid different houses in the middle of the night and pounce upon sleeping women and children. Each time the authorities came, they destroyed every little thing that appeared in sight. They would mix rice and wheat, and sometimes even add oil to the mixture. Living in Punjab became hazardous and risky. If anyone objected against the illegal actions of the Punjab police, they were arrested and falsely implicated in an Arms Act case.[26]

Day after day, from village after village, tales full of horror, sorrow and gory details about the rape of women and the killing of people kept emerging. The legacy of insurgency that Operation

Blue Star inspired continues to cast its shadow over the women of 1984 even today.

After Operation Blue Star, Bibi Rajinder Kaur, the head of the Istri Akali Dal, condemned it and demanded the reopening of the Golden Temple. In response to her call, on 16 July 1984, over a hundred women from various villages—the Shahedi Jatha—came out in droves, courting arrest. Punjab was once again put under curfew. But Bibi Rajinder Kaur stood her ground. Kiranjot Kaur, Bibi Rajinder Kaur's daughter and also a member of the SGPC, told me, 'I asked my mother, what if they shoot you? She said, so then we will be martyrs. My kids are able to look after themselves. They don't need me to take care of them.'

A lady from Fatehgarh Churian later told Kiranjot Kaur that her mother was a part of the group called Shaheedi Jatha. This was a time when the Sikh women, struggling as they were to manage the best they could in the aftermath of devastation, stood up, united in their grief and determination for justice.

A protest song from this movement defines the stories of the women in this book:

Indira sadi datri, assi Indira de soye
Jeon Jeon Indra Wad di, assi doon sawaye hoye
Indira is our axe, we are the grass
As she cuts us down, we will grow in doubles

2
Chaurasi ki Na Insafi

31 October 1984

On Prime Minister Indira Gandhi's schedule for the day was an interview with British actor Peter Ustinov, who was filming a documentary on her for an Irish television channel. Clad in an orange saree, with a black umbrella to protect her from the sun, the prime minister walked from her residence to her office. Two Sikh bodyguards were on duty that morning: Beant Singh and Satwant Singh. Of the two, Indira had known Beant Singh the longest, for well over a decade. He had been taken off her staff duty after Operation Blue Star, but she had insisted that he be allowed to return to his original duties. Satwant Singh was twenty-one years old at that time and he had just come back from a long leave which he had spent in his home in Gurdaspur.

As the prime minister opened the small wicket gate that separated her residence from her office, Beant Singh took out his .38 calibre revolver and aimed it directly at her. What happened next has been recorded several times and richly, but the event loses none of its horror in these retellings. Beant Singh fired three bullets at Indira, sending her to the ground and causing her to bleed profusely. Satwant Singh finished things off, firing as many as thirty bullets into the body of the fallen prime minister with his official Sten gun. When the other residents of 1 Safdarjung Road, the prime minister's official residence, rushed out, they found the two unrepentant bodyguards standing over the bloodstained body of Indira Gandhi.

Dropping his gun, Beant Singh declared in Punjabi, '*Main jo karna si, kar dita. Hun tussi kar lo jo karna hai.* I have done what I had to do. Now you do what you have to do.'[1]

A scuffle took place between the two bodyguards and men of the Indo-Tibetan Border Police who were on duty outside the prime minister's residence. More shots were fired, one of which killed Beant Singh. Satwant was hanged four years later along with Kehar Singh, also executed for conspiring in the plot of Indira Gandhi's assassination.

A frantic hunt ensued for the driver of the ambulance that was parked on the premises of the prime minister's official residence at all times. But he was away for his tea break.

With the prime minister losing blood by the second, there was no time to lose. Indira Gandhi was quickly put inside a white Ambassador car with the prime minister's daughter-in-law, Sonia

Gandhi. Rajinder Kumar Dhawan, personal assistant to Gandhi, drove at top speed to the All India Institute of Medical Sciences (AIIMS), with Sonia cradling her mother-in-law's head in her lap.

At AIIMS, it was soon apparent that the team of doctors working on Indira Gandhi was running out of both time and hope. The prime minister was finally declared dead at 2.30 p.m. But the news of her death could not be broken to the rest of the country without the arrival of her son, Rajiv Gandhi, in New Delhi. Rajiv was on tour in West Bengal with the then finance minister Pranab Mukherjee. Urgent messages were sent to Contai, where he was due to give a speech, asking him to return to New Delhi at once.

Rajiv and Pranab Mukherjee were then airlifted from Contai to Calcutta (now Kolkata) from the Kolaghat Thermal Power Station. At Calcutta, a special Indian airlines aircraft was waiting to take them back to New Delhi.

Once they were on board, the discussion about who would be the next prime minister of India started. In a surreal moment, it was unanimously decided, at an altitude of 35,000 feet that too, that Rajiv would be appointed as the next prime minister, albeit without any due process being followed. It was also decided that Indira Gandhi's death would only be announced to the nation after the swearing-in of the next government.

Meanwhile, President Giani Zail Singh returned from Sana'a in North Yemen immediately upon hearing the news. He went straight from the airport to AIIMS where the main gates were already choked by a constantly growing crowd. On hearing rumours about what had happened, Gandhi's supporters, including some Sikhs, had arrived outside the hospital. Slogans and cheers of 'Indira Gandhi *amar rahe*! Long live Indira Gandhi!' filled the air. It was, however, a scene of the briefest unity, because things quickly turned. As Giani Zail Singh's former media advisor, Tarlochan Singh, narrates, when the President was departing after visiting Indira Gandhi at AIIMS, slogans were raised against him as a mob started closing in on his car. It was with great difficulty that the President's security detachment managed to clear the way.[2]

At around 4.30 p.m., the uneasy calm that had prevailed thus far was shattered as some thirty-five to forty men emerged from nowhere and began shoving the Sikhs present to the ground, sending their turbans flying. It all happened very fast, too fast in fact to even ascertain where these men had arrived from. Within seconds, some of the turbans lying on the ground had been set on fire.

At 6 p.m., Rajiv Gandhi was sworn in as the new prime minister of India.

At the other end of Delhi, Darshan Kaur was unaware of what had happened that day in the heart of the city. Darshan lived with her in-laws in Trilokpuri, a nondescript neighbourhood in East Delhi. Trilokpuri had begun as a home for the poor, disadvantaged and socially deracinated people who had been left homeless after a slum-clearing drive by Congress scion, Sanjay Gandhi, for his ambitious beautification project during the Emergency in 1976.

'Our house was a small one at the corner of the entrance of Block 32,' Darshan told me as she recounted what had happened. 'I lived with my husband, children, parents-in-law, two sisters-in-law and a brother-in-law and his family. It had been a normal day. My husband was a tailor by profession, and he was completing an order that he had to deliver next week. My mother-in-law was helping him pack it. I was in the kitchen, preparing dinner for the family when someone knocked on the door. My mother-in-law asked me to open the door. It was my brother, holding a box of sweets. He came in and sat down next to my mother-in-law. He had come to invite us all for a function to celebrate the birth of his daughter.'

Darshan recalls how her mother-in-law started mocking her brother, saying, 'Why are you celebrating her birth? What's there to celebrate? Keep that money for her dowry.'

Ignoring these snide remarks, Darshan's brother asked her to come that evening to help with the preparations. But this plan was stymied when her brother's sister-in-law, who was also Darshan's neighbour, dropped by to suggest that they should all go together the next day. Darshan's husband also convinced her that it would be better to go with everyone else the next day.

After having a cup of tea, Darshan's brother went back, leaving his sister to finish making dinner and then pack the gifts she had bought for her newborn niece.

During the course of our interviews from 2014 to 2017, whenever she talked to me, Darshan would keep playing with her dupatta and would studiously avoid making eye contact with me. It was obvious that these conversations were hard for her. Every few minutes, she would dab her eyes with her dupatta. There were long pauses in between when she lost herself in her memories and regrets. I tried not to look at her. Her memories were private, and as much as she would let me in, it was a privilege to be made privy to them. During one of these silences, Darshan's daughter-in-law came into the room bearing a tray of tea and some savouries. I have known Darshan for years, and in all the time I have spent with her, she has never let me leave her house without eating something or at least having a cup of tea.

We went back in time again that day as we sipped the tea slowly and Darshan resumed her story.

The next morning, on 1 November, she woke up to finish her household chores so that she could leave on time for the function at her brother's home. At around 10 a.m., she stepped out for a moment to buy a box of matches from the grocery shop down the road.

It was then that she saw the men standing in oddly menacing-looking groups across the road. They were all dressed in white kurta-pyjamas and were armed with lathis, iron rods and other weapons.

'I was terrified. I first thought that maybe it was some kind of a gang war, the way they show in films.'

As she stood there, however, she realized that these men were not actually strangers. They were her neighbours! Then, she became aware of the police presence in the neighbourhood. She heard one of the policemen demanding of the group, 'Why are you standing here? Are you afraid of the Sikhs? Just go and kill all the Sardars.'

As she phrased it in her conversation with me, '… the earth around me shook.'

Petrified, Darshan turned and began running back towards her house. She fell twice on the uneven road, breaking the strap of one of her chappals as she did so. Hampered by the broken strap, she kicked off her chappals and began running barefoot. Looking over her shoulder, she saw that the men had entered her colony and were coming directly towards Block 32.

Breathless and frightened, Darshan barged into her house, calling for her mother-in-law. She told the older woman everything that she had seen and heard, and both of them ran to the rooftop. Spirals of smoke were already visible at a distance—a gurdwara nearby was on fire. They looked down towards the end of their narrow lane and saw that the mob had managed to lay its hands on a middle-aged Sikh man and was beating him with lathis. Panicking, Darshan's mother-in-law told her to go back downstairs and ask her husband to hide. The main door to their house was not to be opened at any cost. 'My brother-in-law was not at home. He had gone out to buy groceries,' Darshan remembered, tears filling her eyes as she narrated the story. 'But my mother-in-law was so scared about what might happen to him that she went out to find him. She looked for him everywhere, but she just couldn't find him. By the time she came back home, she was gasping for breath. She asked all the women and children of the house to come and sit outside, thinking perhaps that we could prevent the mob from entering our homes if we did so.'

Her mother-in-law then rubbed mud on Darshan's face and covered her head with a dupatta. When Darshan tried to stop her from doing so, her mother-in-law shot back roughly, '*Randi, yeh haramzaade le jayenge tujhe!* Whore, these bastards will take you away!' No sooner had she finished rubbing the mud on Darshan's face, than a group of four to five men reached their doorstep. They were looking for Darshan's husband. Darshan recognized a local leader, Rampal Saroj, among the men. He demanded, 'Where is Ram Singh?'

'I told him that I didn't know anything apart from the fact that he had gone out with his brother,' said Darshan.

Saroj assured Darshan that Ram Singh would not be hurt. If anything, Saroj said, he was there to protect Ram Singh rather than harm him. But Darshan refused to budge. Rampal Saroj left then, but he returned a few minutes later with a group of almost fifteen people. The men overpowered Darshan and her mother-in-law and broke open the main door of their house. They found her husband hiding in the kitchen and dragged him out by his hair. They placed a quilt and a tyre over his head, doused him in oil and then set him ablaze. Ram Singh was nearly burnt to death; he later succumbed to his injuries.

Tears now pouring out of her eyes, Darshan continued, 'I saw my husband crying and begging for help, but the mob was merciless. They never allowed us to help. I watched him die.' Darshan believes that this was a mob that did not want to simply murder the Sikhs. 'They also wanted us to witness it all in order to brutalize and scar us forever.'

But this was not the end of their trauma. Right outside her house, Darshan saw her brother-in-law running for his life while a mob of attackers pursued him with swords and sticks. In the ensuing scuffle, he was left bleeding on the ground, his stomach cut open. Desperate and not knowing what else to do, Darshan and her mother-in-law tied their dupattas around his open stomach. She recalled him begging for water, but there was no water to give him. Her mother-in-law sat numbly beside her son, staring at the sky; the brightness of the sun at such a dark hour was too much for her to bear. Around her lay the bodies of her sons—one burnt to death and the other dying by degrees. Darshan tried to speak to her, and almost as though she was galvanized by the sound of her voice, her mother-in-law began hitting her stomach and tearing at her hair. 'She was absolutely devastated.'

In the winter of 1984, Trilokpuri became a burial ground, the air rent by smoke and inhuman screams. 'The mob did not even spare the dead,' Darshan told me. 'They removed gold rings and chains from the dead bodies. They were not scared of the law.' It was as if the mob had been clearly instructed and perhaps even given some kind of training in what to do before the massacre. In the midst of this chaos, women were forced out of their homes by the attackers who wanted to prevent them from giving any assistance to their male kith and kin; most of those who were milling around on the streets were women. Those who tried to intervene and save their fathers, husbands, sons and brothers were attacked brutally by the marauding mob. Darshan heard Rampal Saroj instigating the mob, shouting, 'No one should be spared!' She was not spared either. The mob dragged her down the road before pushing her to the ground. During this ordeal, she was separated from her twenty-day-old son, while her eldest son, a toddler of four, was attacked by arsonists with an iron rod; her son still bears a visible mark of the attack. When she pleaded with her attackers to spare her son, they called him the child of a snake.

At about 4 p.m., after the mob had murdered all the Sikh men they could get hold of in Block 32, they instructed all the women seated outside their homes. 'Now your men are dead. Come out and sit together in the park nearby Block 32.' The women came out and all huddled together. The mobsters offered them some water, but no one drank it. Then the men began dragging off whichever girl caught their fancy. 'Each girl was taken by a gang of some ten or twelve men. Many of these girls were in their teens. They would be taken to nearby shelters, raped and then sent back after a few hours,' Darshan recalled. 'The men were monsters. They also raped women who were of their mother's and grandmother's ages.'

Some girls never came back, and those who did were in a pitiable condition, naked and bruised. Darshan recalled how a young girl of about fifteen came back sobbing—she had been raped multiple times by men as old as her grandfather. Guddi[3] (name changed), a woman in her late fifties, was raped in front of all the other women. Darshan remembered the scene with painful clarity, 'She was crying throughout, but the monsters did not stop. They took turns on her. Men as young as seventeen raped her. When they left, she was lying on the ground, naked like a newborn. The women in the park covered her with sheets. These rapists were not bothered about anything. After all, they had unsaid police permissions.' Darshan added, 'The leaders of the Congress Party were coming and dragging women to nearby houses too.'

In less than two hours, there were 275 widows across 180 homes. In an area less than 1,000 sq. yards, hundreds of limbless bodies were scattered about.[4] Worse was the fact that none of them knew why this was happening in the first place. All the women were sitting numbly when they heard the mob shouting, '*Netaji aa gaye hain*! Our leader has come!' Darshan pushed through the women and saw Congress leader H.K.L. Bhagat stepping down from his gleaming white Ambassador. He was clad in a white kurta-pyjama, with dark sunglasses over his eyes. He received a warm welcome from the same men who had been murdering and raping the Sikh inhabitants of Block 32 only a short while ago. 'I thought he was there to save us. But when he stepped down from his white car, he told the crowd that Indira Gandhi was their mother and these Sikhs had killed their mother,' said Darshan. She told me that she heard H.K.L. Bhagat saying, 'Whatever you need—chemicals, kerosene, petrol or anything—I will give to you. Not a single child of these Sardars should survive. They have killed our mother, Indira Gandhi.'

That was the first time that Darshan realized that Indira Gandhi was dead.

'I felt my grandmother's pain at that time. She walked from Pakistan to India, searching for a place she could call home. She thought she would be safe in India. But are we? We were no less than refugees in our own country. We were abandoned. We never mattered.'

3
Sultanpuri

Satwant Kaur[1] was only sixteen when she married her husband, an autorickshaw driver. Tall and cheerful, Satwant was the eldest among her eight siblings, and as a young girl, she had harboured dreams of becoming a singer like Lata Mangeshkar. Once, on her way back from the school, Satwant remembers seeing a large crowd gathered in an open space near Fatehpuri Station. There were huge posters of a woman standing on a stage with a microphone in her hand. There were people sitting on the ground and quite a few who were standing atop the roofs of the buses nearby. There was a lot of noise and the police was trying to control the crowd. After some time, an orchestra started playing some music and within minutes, the cheering crowd went silent as the magical voice of Lata Mangeshkar soared out, enthralling them all. Satwant was thirteen years old and when she saw the crowd swaying to Lata Mangeshkar's songs, she couldn't stop herself from climbing up onto the roof of a bus. She was so mesmerized by the singer that she hoped she could also become a singer like her one day. But her real life turned out to be very different from her dreams.

Satwant's mother was a deeply religious woman who was often wrapped up entirely in prayers and she rarely stepped out of the house. Her father, a block-level leader of the Congress Party, ran a watch repair store in Nangloi. He was also an alcoholic, spending all his money on liquor and contributing next to nothing towards the monthly household expenses. Satwant had wanted to study further after school, but her father wanted her to get married as soon as possible in order to rid himself of being responsible for her.

The young man chosen as a husband for Satwant was a Sikh boy from Bengal, who had come to Delhi in search of a better life after his parents' death. An avid reader, he had wanted to be an engineer, but his personal financial situation led to his taking up the job of an autorickshaw driver. After her marriage, Satwant and her husband settled down temporarily on a plot of land that her parents had gifted the newlyweds, which was next to her father's home. Her father had wanted her to stay close to home. He had reasoned that if Satwant was close by, there would be someone to continue taking care of the cooking and other household chores in his house.

Satwant was comfortable in her new marital home as her husband would get all the necessary supplies for her, although he, too, never gave her any money directly. It did not bother her because there was enough food on the table. But since her husband was not in favour of his wife managing her parents' kitchen with his money, Satwant had to work in order to run her father's kitchen. Her husband, however, did not approve of this, so Satwant decided to do it without telling him. She took up hand embroidery and stitching work, and whatever little money she made, she used for her parents' kitchen. Her father's house was a busy one, given his political position, and on most days, Satwant would spend hours in the kitchen, making endless cups of tea for her father's political friends.

For the first couple of years after their marriage, Satwant and her husband saved as much as they could. They wanted to build a house of their own and also take a trip to Calcutta. Satwant's husband's brother lived in Calcutta, and the two brothers hadn't met for years.

On 31 October 1984, Satwant's husband booked seats on the night train to Sealdah. It would be Satwant's first ever trip out of Delhi, and needless to say, she was terribly excited. She had made pickles and had even knitted a new sweater for her brother-in-law. She had made new sets of clothes for herself as well; she wanted to look her best for this first trip to her in-laws' home in Calcutta. Satwant's reclusive, spiritual mother, meanwhile, was desperately worried about her daughter's safety. Not only would Satwant be travelling with her thirteen-month-old son, but she was also expecting her second child. On the afternoon of 31 October, she came to help Satwant prepare some food for the train journey to Calcutta.

At around 5 p.m., Satwant went to the bedroom where her husband was sleeping. She woke him up and asked him to buy some sweets for their relatives in Calcutta. Her husband asked her for a cup of tea first, saying he would go to the market after having the tea. He was still in bed when she returned with a hot cup of tea. 'I was standing close to his bed with the tray in my hand. He asked me to put the tray on the table and then he pulled my hand, forcing me to bend down. I could hear his heart beating. He kissed my forehead, but he said nothing,' recalled Satwant.

Before he left, Satwant's husband told her to be ready to leave for the station when he got back. 'He said he would be back in ten minutes.'

She did as he had asked, quickly finishing the last bits of packing and then locking up the house and standing outside with her infant son, her mother and their luggage. Mother and daughter were talking to each other when they saw an old woman running towards them. Her hair was flying wild around her and she had barely any clothes on. She was screaming, 'I have lost everything. What will I do now? Where will I go?' Alarmed and petrified, Satwant ran to the old woman and caught hold of her hand. She asked the woman what had happened. 'All the men in my family have been killed,' the old woman sobbed. 'My husband and son have been burnt to death by the mob.'

Just as she finished telling her tale of horror, Satwant saw a phalanx of armed men entering the colony. They were attacking whoever tried to stop them or bar their way. It was clear that they were looking for Sikh men, women and children; she could see them beating up the Sikhs they could grab. Before the mob could reach the spot where the paralysed Satwant was standing, her neighbours—a family from Rajasthan—ran out and pulled Satwant, her son and mother inside their house. Hastily, they pulled out some traditional Rajasthani attire and handed it to her. She was asked to change into the clothes and sit outside in the courtyard with the other women of the family. The men, warned by the noise and the chaos outside, stood guarding the house.

Satwant recalled how as she sat in the courtyard with her infant son, she was terrified for her husband and the other members of her family. Her father was a local Congress leader, but she knew that that fact would not help him. The mob was not concerned with his politics as much as it was concerned with his identity. He was a Sikh, and they were out to get as many Sikhs as they could lay their hands on. Meanwhile, absolutely petrified by what she had witnessed, Satwant's mother ran home to her family. She untied her young sons' hair and tied neat ponytails instead. The little boys were then dressed in their sisters' frocks to make it seem like theirs was a home of little girls. Satwant's father had somehow managed to escape from the house, taking refuge in the home of a Dalit butcher's family nearby. It was this Dalit family that would save his life. They hid Satwant's father inside a pit where they kept their pigs, and when the mob finally turned up at their doorstep looking for him, they refused to allow the men to enter. They insisted that there was no such Sikh man on the premises. To reinforce their point, the men of the family picked up the meat cleavers of their trade and came out, armed to the teeth. The elderly matriarch of the household also came out running with an axe in her hand. 'Before laying your hands on him, you will have to go through all of us,' she threatened. Furious, the mob set fire to Satwant's parents' home instead.

Satwant was sitting in the veranda of her neighbour's house when she saw the flames going up from her parents' and her newly constructed one-room house. Unable to control herself, she ran towards the house. The other women tried to stop her, but they all failed. She recalled begging her neighbours for help, but nobody came forth. As she desperately looked around for a bucket in which she could fill water, Satwant was suddenly seized by a man who had been watching her from across the road. He pushed her roughly, causing her to trip and fall to her knees.

'I lay there helplessly, watching my home go up in flames. I thought of going inside to get the money out of my trunk, but within minutes, everything fell apart. My house was gutted, and so were all my hopes. I was trying to get up and go inside the burning house to save whatever I could, but I was unable to stand up. My legs felt numb. An old woman tried to help me. But she was warned loudly of the consequences of protecting a Sikh woman.'

And then, a van pulled up and its occupants pulled Satwant inside.

'I was two months pregnant. A few minutes later, I was in an open byre. It was in the home of one of the men who raped me. I could clearly hear the women of the house talking to each other, calling their kids. I thought that if I shouted, maybe someone would come and rescue me. But before I could do so, an old lady shouted, "Don't leave these whores. They killed our mother. They will produce more snakes."

'They were four of them taking turns on me. When I protested, they started to hit me. Once I was raped, I was left with no strength to fight back. They were laughing and discussing all the other women they had been eyeing. I was raped multiple times. They left me there and went out to get other women. I was in so much pain that I could hardly move. I was lying on the ground, bleeding.

'While I was lying there, I remember thinking that maybe it was my fault. Maybe, I had somehow tempted them. Maybe I wasn't wearing the right clothes. I was numb, thinking about what I could do now. Those monsters had scarred me for life. How could I show my face to my husband and my child? Society would never accept me. I was crying and looking at the sky.'

There in the byre, Satwant lay naked and bleeding on the ground while other women were brought in and raped. 'My eyes were wide open,' Satwant recalled. 'I remember how tears just kept streaming down my face. I didn't know anything, but I kept mumbling the words to the song "*Zindagi pyaar ka geet hai*".'

Eventually though, Satwant found the strength to get up and walk back home in the same state as she had been left on the ground: naked. 'On my way back, women were looking at me and some were laughing at me. I don't exactly remember how many men touched me on my way back, but one phrase I clearly remember hearing was "*Dekh, randi ki chaal.* Look, a whore's walk." These words didn't come from the men. They came from the women. I would say that humanity died that day. I was raped collectively—by the entire Congress government. All of them, including the prime minister, President, home minister and, in fact, everyone in this country who failed to protect us.'

Only when she reached her neighbourhood did the women she knew come running with bedsheets and clothes to cover Satwant's naked body. Yet again, her neighbours from Rajasthan came to her rescue, bringing her fresh clothes and sheltering her inside their home. 'Women who resisted rape, who argued with the men, they were all killed.'

When things became quiet Satwant set out to her parents' home and her one-room set, but all she found were the remnants of smouldering wooden logs. Everything had turned to ash. She had no clue where her parents or siblings were. She was worried to death for her young son; she had been separated from him in the chaos and confusion of the entire situation. Of her husband there was no sign. His half-burnt auto was found two weeks later.

As Satwant told me this story, her eyes were full of unshed tears. In between, as she paused to recollect and remember everything that had happened, she would hum, almost subconsciously, the words to an old Bollywood song, '*Aate jaate khoobsurat awara galliyon mein kabhi kabhi ...*' Then, suddenly remembering where she was and what she was doing, she would laugh and continue talking, as though nothing had happened to break the flow of her story. As I listened to her, I tried not to feel afraid myself.

The Sikhs of Sultanpuri were Sikligar Sikhs, beloved traditional weapon makers. This community had withstood the onslaught of the Mughals and the British, but the pogrom of 1984 shattered them in ways they are still only just beginning to identify. The landscape of Delhi has changed in the last three decades with metro lines crisscrossing the city and a boom in infrastructural advancement. Yet, in these settlements, in Sultanpuri, nothing has changed. These communities still live in fear. As Satwant told me, 'I thought all of this will end soon and everything will be normal shortly. But it's been thirty years. I'm still waiting for things to get back to normal.'

4

Raj Nagar

In 1984, Nirpreet Kaur was sixteen years old.
Of all the memories of her youth, the clearest one is of running after a raging mob and trying to prevent it from setting her father on fire.

'I saw my father dying at the hands of the mob during the 1984 Sikh massacre. I couldn't sleep for so many months afterwards. Whenever I would try to close my eyes, that scene of the mob trying to immolate my father would appear in front of my eyes, again and again.

'Before 31 October 1984, we were living happily in Raj Nagar, in Delhi's Palam Colony. My father Nirmal Singh owned a taxi stand and ran a successful transport business in Delhi, while my mother Sampuran Kaur was a homemaker. I had two younger brothers, Nirpal and Nirmolak Singh. The events of the day when

Mrs Gandhi was assassinated are still fresh in my mind. My father came home around four in the evening, breathless and in a state of panic.

'That evening, Balwan Singh Khokhar, nephew of Councillor Sajjan Kumar,[1] visited our home along with his brother Kishan Khokhar. They came to meet my father. Balwan Singh wanted to know if my father could give his brother a taxi to drive. Papa was a worried man that evening. He asked Balwan Singh to give him some time to find out about the availability of a taxi.

'Meanwhile, Karnail Singh, who lived two lanes behind our house, was passing by when he saw my father and his guests and stopped. My father asked him how things were outside and Karnail Singh replied that everything was tense; there were mobs burning shops and vehicles. Karnail Singh then asked my father why he had returned so early. "What about your taxis?" he enquired. To this my father said, "I have safely parked the ones which are in Delhi, and may God be with the ones which have gone out for a trip."

'At that point, Balwan Singh told Papa not to worry. He said that he would try his best to protect our family and everyone in Raj Nagar. He said that if required, he would personally ask his uncle Sajjan Kumar for help. But I think the real reason he came to see us that evening was to check if the Sikhs in Raj Nagar had heard of the mobs roaming outside and whether or not they were prepared to defend their homes.'

The next day, in the early hours of the morning, Nirpreet saw a mob trying to forcibly enter the neighbourhood gurdwara. Among the men were Mahinder Yadav, Balwan Singh Khokhar and Kishan Singh Khokar. Without wasting any time, Nirpreet ran to the gurdwara and managed to extricate the copy of the Guru Granth Sahib that was kept there. But as she was sneaking out from the back door of the gurdwara, her nine-year-old brother, who had accompanied her, was seized by the mob. She then heard Mahinder Yadav yell, '*Isse bhi maaro! Yeh saap ka bachaa hai.* Kill him too! He is an offspring of a snake.' Nirpreet continued running with the Guru Granth Sahib on her head, while her brother managed to escape, although he did catch some brutal blows from the lathi-carrying mob.

When she reached home, Nirpreet saw that the boundary wall of their home had been broken and the mob had moved on to torching the shops nearby. The family's scooter was parked right in front of their home, but the mob was not bothered about the scooter. They were interested in Nirpreet who was carrying the holy book on her head. Nirpreet began screaming, and her screams prompted her thirteen-year-old brother to pick up a sword and come running to try and disperse the gathering crowd. It was then that Nirpreet saw them.

Balwan Singh Khokhar, along with Mahinder Yadav, were at the forefront of the aggressive crowd and they were locked in a confrontation with her father, who was demanding to know what had happened to the previous evening's promise of safety. Balwan Singh responded to Nirmal Singh's questions with aggression.

'My father begged the crowd to understand that we hadn't killed Indira Gandhi. He said, "Why are you coming after us? You have burnt the gurdwara and attacked my daughter and wife, but what have they done? If you want blood, kill me, but leave them alone." Khokhar then intervened and asked the crowd to move along.'

But Balwan Singh Khokhar was not finished with Nirpreet's father just yet.

A few hours later, in the lull that followed that first attack, a truck parked outside Nirpreet's home was burnt. Her father then asked all the Sikh families living in the two lanes of Palam Colony to get ready to fight in order to protect themselves.

'We fought for four hours with the mob,' recalled Nirpreet, 'and in this fight some people from the mob also got injured. When the mob realized that the Sikhs were overpowering them, Balwan Khokhar and Mahinder Yadav came to our home again. They were with the police this time. They asked us why we were fighting. "We are brothers, let's compromise," they said to my father.

'My father said, "What compromise? You have attacked Gurdwara Sahib, my wife is unconscious, and you have burnt a truck in front of my house." One of the policemen standing there then said to my father, "Sardar ji, it's better to compromise. Your children have extricated the Guru Granth Sahib from the gurdwara." It struck me then that they had been watching us. They pressurized my father into agreeing to a compromise and took away all our lathis and kirpans. They basically unarmed us. They pressured my father into compromising and deceived him into leaving his home. One of our neighbours, Mohan Uncle, said that my father will not return now, and the moment he said that, I ran after my father.

'The mob was standing a little distance away from us, and I saw Balwan Singh push my father right into the hands of the mob and say, "*Yeh jo sardar tum chorh aaye the, main le aaya hoon.* This sardar that you had left behind, I have brought him."

'What happened next is something that I watched with helpless horror because I was forcibly held back from running to my father. Ishwarchand Sharabi handed over the kerosene to be sprinkled on my father and when the mob was unable to find any matchsticks, a policeman standing there—his name was Inspector Kaushik—gave a matchbox to Kishan Khokhar. Khokhar set my father on fire. Papa jumped into a drain to try and save himself, but he was pulled out, tied to a pole and set on fire a second time.'

Nirpreet's memories of that morning are graphic and disturbing. 'My father fought them off and jumped into the drain again. I saw a priest from the local temple call upon the mob to hit Papa on the head with a rod. So Balwan Khokhar hit him with a rod and Mahendra Yadav sprinkled some white powder on him.'

Nirpreet doesn't know for sure what that powder was. She alleges it was white phosphorous, a deadly chemical which caused her father's skin to burn fatally and which gave him an eventual, agonizing death. However, she wasn't the first person to mention this white powder. Several of the women that I spoke to during the course of my research for this book told me about a similar white powder, which burns human flesh and which catches fire when exposed to the air, both properties of white phosphorous.

Nirpreet and what was left of her family moved in with Wing Commander L.S. Pannu, who, on 2 November, a day after Nirmal Singh's death, provided them with a vehicle and offered them the services of Air Force jawans to go to Palam Colony. He also asked her to bring the other Sikhs residing in the area back to the Air Force Station.

Nirpreet went back and the first thing she did was to go and collect her father's ashes for his last rites. But she couldn't find anything at all. The entire area had been swept clean. Congress leader Sajjan Kumar was making a speech when she got there. 'Sajjan Kumar was saying that not a single Sikh who killed Indira Gandhi should be saved,' Nirpreet told me. The atmosphere was electric and the jawans accompanying Nirpreet asked her to not proceed any further. They returned quietly to the Air Force Station in Palam.

A few days later, on 5 November, Balwan Khokhar came directly to the Air Force Station, bringing, with calm audacity, milk and biscuits for the victims sheltering inside. He asked about the whereabouts of Nirmal Singh's family. There is no knowing what would have happened had someone not identified him as the person responsible for the killings in Delhi Cantonment. Balwan managed to flee the base, but it wasn't over for Nirpreet and her family.

Nirpreet and her mother started receiving threats, alleging that they were being too dangerously outspoken and vocal about what had happened. Terrified and with their lives constantly in peril, they lived like nomads in a city that had once been their home, hiding in different locations and moving from place to place before finally settling down in a rented accommodation in West Delhi's Tilak Vihar. Even here, however, they were not safe and were constantly harassed by Sajjan Kumar's goons and by the Delhi Police.

'When Sajjan Kumar was given a ticket to contest elections for the Parliament in December 1984, I lost all faith in the judicial process. Instead, I swore to avenge my father's killing.'

This is the first time that Nirpreet Kaur has put words to the memories of what happened during that winter morning in 1984. Having lost her father, the young Delhi University student transitioned from the realm of pens to the resolute embrace of militant ideals.

5

Mukherjee Nagar

It has been over thirty years since it happened, yet Nirmal Kaur still looks frightened at the memory of that night. The details, when she begins recounting them, are chilling.

'A group of over 100 people wearing red shirts and black pants marched towards our house. Some of them were carrying torches. When they reached our house, we could hear them question our Punjabi tenants on the ground floor and ask if any Sikh family lived on the first floor. Our tenants said no. But despite their denial, the mob persistently asked them to hand over the Sardar family that lived upstairs. I was only fifteen then. My parents had sent me and my siblings to our neighbours' house just a little earlier. We had leapt from the first floor, and our neighbours were standing with bedsheets held open as safety nets, allowing us to land safely. They promised us safety and refuge. We could see our parents waiting for the inevitable. They were crying and shivering, torn between relief over their children's safety and fear as they looked at the mob which wanted to kill us all.' Nirmal told me that though they were asking questions, the mob knew the family's whereabouts.

'They wanted to set our car on fire, but some of them suggested that they burn down the Sikh gurdwara first. Much to our surprise, the mob turned away from our house and went towards the gurdwara. After they were done looting and pilfering the gurdwara, they left our street and marched on to the next street,' she added.

There, Nirmal said, they attacked other Sikh families, harassed women and tried to cut off the hair of Sikh boys. They set fire to rubber tyres and threw them over innocent Sikh boys, engulfing them in flames. When I asked her if she still felt scared today, she replied, 'Even today, my mother panics if a door is slammed too hard. She cannot help but cry when she is asked about these events. I, too, feel horrified remembering that night. Those who saved us were Hindus. My cousin sister and her kids were saved by a Muslim family that let them stay with them for almost a week.'

While recording Nirmal's story, I saw tears fill her eyes again and again. In fact, often while recording a survivor's statement, I would see their eyes well up. Tears would roll down their cheeks, but most of them never realized they were crying.

Today, Nirmal Kaur seems more anguished than scared. Her family lost neither property nor money during the pogrom of 1984, but they did lose hope in a system that should have been on their side.

Nirmal Kaur now lives with her family in Patiala. She never wants to return to Delhi.

6
Hondh

In Hondh Chillar, a village in the Rewari district of Haryana, a mass grave of Sikhs was unearthed in 2010, twenty-six years after the anti-Sikh massacre. It was a chance discovery by Manvinder Singh Giaspuria, a textile engineer for a company based in Gurugram.

One day, while on his way to deliver a scheduled consignment, he had happened to fall into a conversation with a driver. During the course of their chat, the driver told Manvinder about a deserted Sikh village near the Pataudi-Rewari road. Manvinder decided to go and see the village for himself the next day.

I met Manvinder at his residence in Ludhiana in 2016. Recalling his visit, Manvinder said, 'We could see the ruins of Hondh village the moment we entered it. Hondh used to be a dhani,[1] it comprised havelis and farmhouses of some influential

Sikhs who had migrated from Pakistan during 1947. The road running right up to Hondh was once a pucca road. But now it is wildly overgrown on both sides. No one has been walking on those footpaths for years now. There was a burnt down haveli at the very beginning of the road. A few of the buildings even had some bones scattered inside them. It was all very frightening and haunting.'

I visited Hondh the same year with a photographer friend. The site was a chilling one, nothing less than a graveyard. We saw the remnants of a gurdwara, even though it was in ruins. Yet another remarkable sight was the local mosque, built before Partition and left untouched during the violence of 1984. While we were exploring the village, a white Mahindra Scorpio pulled up at the entrance to the village. Its driver, a man wearing a tie-dyed turban and a white kurta, called out to us. In a clearly aggressive tone, he began asking us questions about what we were doing there and why. He then asked us to leave immediately. When I refused, he made a call on his cellphone and within minutes, a group of men appeared. Their intentions were plain.

My friend rushed back to our car and, leaping in, started the ignition, shouting my name all the while. I kept refusing to leave, but when I looked into the man's eyes directly for the first time, I froze. The next thing I felt was my friend dragging me backwards to the car. Pushing me in, he got into the driver's seat and put the car in reverse. We backed down the village road for half a mile before we hit the highway.

The next day, I called the police to report what had happened. They asked me not to worry and invited us to visit Hondh again and, in fact, connected me with people in the village.

Hondh was attacked on 2 November 1984, at around 11 a.m. as per the copy of First Information Report (FIR) No. 91 presented in the Punjab and Haryana High Court. 'They were determined to eliminate Sikhs from the Dhani (Hojipur) because those Sikhs had killed our beloved leader Indira Gandhi,' reads the statement recorded by the complainant in the FIR.

As per the FIR, the marauders came from Haily Mandi, a market town in Pataudi. They were initially calmed down by the locals of Chillar village, who convinced them to go back. The mob was almost 400-men strong at that point in time, prompting villagers from neighbouring Nurpur village to also come and try to ease the situation. They were, however, brushed aside with the words, 'These Sikhs are traitors. We will finish them.' Although the mob eventually left, the men returned after sunset, this time in bigger numbers. On that night alone, thirty-two people were killed. Multiple homes were set on fire, as was a gurdwara. Bodies were so badly burnt that even the locals could not identify them. Men and children were beaten and thrown into the burning houses. Women were first raped and then thrown into the fires. Nobody came to claim the corpses. The local police conducted a mass funeral for the dead. But their ashes were never claimed, and were thrown instead either into the nearby well or into the neighbouring fields.

During our conversation, Manvinder also mentioned an eyewitness who had told him that the mob had also killed a toddler by slamming the little body several times against a wall.

The massacre in Hondh was a planned attack to uproot the flourishing Sikh business community. The surviving Sikhs escaped in a tractor trolley to Rewari under the cover of night and found shelter there. The survivors now reside in Ludhiana and Bathinda in Punjab. They have sold their land in Hondh for nominal prices and don't intend to return to the village because they are still too scared to do so.

Manvinder Singh Giaspuria was asked to leave his company after he exposed the mass graves in Hondh. Today, he lives in Ludhiana with his family and continues to support the survivors of the anti-Sikh massacre of 1984. Giaspuria won the Punjab assembly elections in 2022 and is now an MLA from Payal constituency near Ludhiana.

7
November 1984

In 2016, I went to Chandigarh to meet Dr Gurdeep Kaur, the daughter of the late Giani Zail Singh, the President of India in 1984. In my interview with her, Dr Kaur told me, 'We were scared and felt threatened during 1984. My father rang the then home minister, P.V. Narasimha Rao, to call the army in for help. He rang up the prime minister's office as well, but his calls were either not getting through or were being disconnected. My father was not briefed by the prime minister on the situation. The police were not helping the Sikhs. It all looked organized, even the commissions said so. Sadly, there was no timely action by the then government.'

I also met the former chief justice of Delhi High Court, Justice Rajinder Sachar, in 2016 at the conclave organized by Amnesty International at the India Habitat Centre in New Delhi. My report on the anti-Sikh massacres of 1984 was being released at this conclave. When I asked him about the pogrom of 1984, Justice Sachar told me, 'Soon after the assassination of Mrs Gandhi on 31 October, when almost all of Delhi was burning, an opposition MP rang up the newly inducted home minister, P.V. Narsimha Rao, to inform him about the situation in the city and the need for the army to be called in. He said that curfew should be imposed. On the afternoon of 1 November, several citizens, including senior government officials, went to meet the President of India. They were told that the government was still considering whether or not to call in the army; regardless, till late night, there were no signs of curfew even as mobs wreaked havoc in the national capital.'

The mobs that Justice Sachar spoke to me of were indeed running amok through the streets of Delhi in 1984, equipped with iron rods, cans of petrol and kerosene and an execution plan: first, gurdwaras would be desecrated. Second, Sikh establishments would be identified, looted and burnt down. And third, any Sikhs caught alive would be bludgeoned to death. This was a pattern of attack that would reverberate across the city and build into a genocide. Most of the victims belonged to lower-income backgrounds and they lived in jhuggi-jhopadi (slum) colonies in the trans-Yamuna area. The localities worst affected by the violence were Block 32 in Trilokpuri, Sultanpuri, Mangolpuri and Seemapuri. The Sikhs in these areas were mostly daily wagers while the women were homemakers. These colonies were targeted because they were enclosed and easily identifiable. The Sikhs, especially the men, were brutally murdered—their necks were ringed with tyres that were filled with either petrol or kerosene oil and they were then set on fire. Their wives, mothers, sisters and daughters were raped. Thousands of children were left orphaned.

From Karol Bagh to Moti Bagh, from Connaught Place to Chandni Chowk, anything that belonged to the Sikhs, be it commercial properties or vehicles, fell prey to the mobs that went on a rampage across the national capital.

Senior journalist Harminder Kaur, who lived in Bhogal in South Delhi at that time, told me that throughout the morning of 1 November, there was an influx of armed men from outside Delhi. They were brought in, she said, on government buses, in jeeps and in trucks—all with one mission: to butcher the Sikhs. 'Hundreds of men were brought in from Bahadurgarh even though the state borders were sealed. Posh localities and neighbourhoods like Maharani Bagh and New Friends Colony were engulfed in the conflagration of the massacre; mobs roamed about with lists bearing addresses of properties owned by Sikhs.'

Several calls for help were made to police control rooms. None were answered.

'In desperation, some Sikhs tuned their radios onto FM and discovered that the only instructions given to the police were to look after Bravo Two's (Rajiv Gandhi's) security and safety.'

In Bhogal, continued Harminder Kaur, the fear was such that even her brothers didn't venture out of the house for days. She had to go out furtively to get supplies for the family. 'Perhaps we were lucky that our neighbours stood up for us. The Afghans in the neighbourhood showed the locals how to make petrol bombs and that helped the Sikhs defend their lives and properties.'

In 2016, at the same conclave where I met Justice Sachar, Seema Mustafa, a senior journalist who had been working with the *Telegraph* in 1984, said to me, 'It was a complete bonfire—around the Parliament, the area which is the VVIP area, around the Rashtrapati Bhavan, around South Block and North Block, that whole area ... All that you could see were the huge fires rising up from the Sikh taxi stands that were being burnt. In South Delhi, I actually saw with my own eyes, mobs entering houses that they knew belonged to Sikhs and dragging people out. Some were saved. But many were not saved. I went to Trilokpuri with a photographer. There were not many journalists out there. Remember that this was the time before television. Except for one or two newspapers, the other papers did not flood Delhi with their reporters, so actual eyewitnesses were few and far between. You can count them on your fingers.'

Mustafa recalled that when she arrived in Trilokpuri, chaos was prevailing. 'We had borrowed someone's old white Ambassador, and we were wondering why people were running. Then we realized that the entire place was burning. We stopped the car and got out to see what was being burnt. To our shock, we realized they were human bodies. Each bonfire had bodies.'

To get a rough count of how many victims there were, Mustafa remembers stopping by each bonfire and counting the number of bodies she could see.

'People often referred to rumours, deadly rumours, that it was the Sikhs who were butchering people. One of the rumours circulating at that time was that trains were coming in from Punjab, loaded with dead bodies. This was an unmistakable parallel being drawn between the trains of 1984 and those that came from Pakistan during Partition. I went to the railway station very early in the morning—I must have been there at 7 a.m. and I was there till six or seven in the evening. I was the only reporter there—and there were trains coming in and all of them *were* full of bodies of Sikhs. So, because the rumour going around was that the Sikhs were killing people, Hindu mobs were incited to go to the outskirts of Delhi, stop trains coming in from different locations, pull out the Sikh passengers, burn them alive, and then put their bodies back into the coaches. I counted 200 dead bodies in one day.'

And what of the women? Where were the Kaurs of 1984 while this carnage was taking place? My conversations with the survivors of the massacres reveal a grim timeline.

Between 31 October 1984 and 2 November 1984, Sikh women across Delhi were either hiding or running around the national capital with their children, looking for safety. Those who were caught by the mob were either abducted or raped. Among the women I spoke to, those who had witnessed Partition told me that in their eyes, 1984 was no different from 1947 in the kind of gendered violence that broke out across the capital. Women were at the heart of crimes of revenge and communalism in 1947, and they were at the heart of similar crimes in 1984 as well. Their own families brutalized them too, by forcing them to stay silent in order to safeguard the chastity and purity of the family, thinking who would marry these girls if the truth became known.

Harminder Kaur told me, 'No effort was made to contain violence in the Congress (I) ruled states until Mrs Gandhi was cremated on 3 November 1984. Until the cremation, even Doordarshan allowed a free run of slogans like "*Khoon ka badla khoon se lenge*! We will avenge blood with blood!" Deadly rumours were afloat to whip up frenzy against the community.'[1]

Against this bloodied backdrop, journalists like Kaur and Mustafa both faced an ethical and moral dilemma of sorts. What was happening across the city was not just unprecedented and tragic, but it would require what Mustafa simply put as 'new rules and new accountability'. The year 1984 would be a ghastly new landmark in modern Indian history, and the language of journalism would need to change in order to report the massacres with humanity.

Given the circumstances, it was a difficult consideration to make, but Mustafa, for one, was decisive in her thinking. 'When I came back to the office (from the railway station), I was sure that this was a landmark change—not just for the country, but for journalism. One of the discussions we had with Calcutta (where the *Telegraph* is headquartered) was whether we should say that 200 Sikhs had been killed or if we should just say 200 killed.[2] This was a time when you never identified a community by its faith. Until now, there had of course been communal massacres, but as journalists, we would not name a particular community. That day, I remember there was a two-hour debate because I was insisting that we use *200 Sikhs*. The minute you say just 200 killed, it would feed into the rumours that the 200 killed were not just Sikhs.'

For Darshan Kaur, from Trilokpuri, the carnage of 1984 brought back the horrors of Partition. 'I felt as if I was one of the characters in my grandmother's Partition stories. She had migrated from Karachi, Pakistan, to India in 1947. The violence of Partition drove my family first to Sadpuri and then to Bharatpur in Alwar, Rajasthan, looking for work and homestead. They were allotted a piece of agricultural land in Bharatpur almost a decade after they left Pakistan as refugees.'

Darshan was born in 1961, into a poor Sikh Labana family. This particular community is more comfortable speaking in Labanki,[3] an extinct Indo-Aryan language which is a mixture of Marwari, Saraiki, Gujarati and Marathi.

On the night of 1 November, Darshan and her mother-in-law took refuge in the shell of a house under construction, which belonged to a member of the Sansi tribe of Rajasthan. 'He allowed us to stay only on the condition that we would leave early the next morning,' recalled Darshan. 'It was a terrible situation. We were numb. I had lost my husband in the morning. My eldest son had been attacked with a rod, my middle son was traumatized and my youngest son, just a few days old, was missing. My tears had dried. We were full of fear. The only thing we wanted then was to get out of that damned place. It was a do-or-die situation. The children were hungry. They were scared and crying, and we had to cover their mouths with our hands so that nobody could hear them. There was nothing that we could have done for them. They eventually fell asleep after crying for some time. Now, looking back, it scares me to think about what would have happened if my boys had also died.'

Early next morning, they were woken up by the man who had given them shelter. He insisted that they vacate his property immediately; he had been warned of the consequences of sheltering Sikhs.

It was a dark winter morning and everything was absolutely still and quiet. Darshan said, 'Trilokpuri Block 32 looked as if no one had ever lived there. It was an open ground. All the houses belonging to the Sikh families had been razed to the ground. The smell of burnt wood and human flesh hung heavy in the air. Dead bodies were everywhere. While you walked through the colony, you could easily stumble over a body or a limb or two. It was a warzone. The stench of the dead was unbearable, but they were our own people. I was thinking to myself that maybe my husband was alive. I had watched him die, but somehow, hope remained. But despite my hope, nobody could have possibly recognized what was left of him. Most of the bodies were limbless and charred. Even war has some rules.'

Her mother-in-law, meanwhile, continued to search for her eldest son who had been grievously injured but alive when they had seen him last. Darshan followed the elder woman to what was left of their home in Block 32. Her brother-in-law was still lying outside on the ground, his stomach cut open. 'He was in immense pain. We could easily see inside his stomach,' remembered Darshan. The two women tried to lift him, but he was too heavy for them and he was obviously dying. Tears streamed down his cheeks as he asked his mother to hold his hand and then begged her to leave as soon as possible to save the rest of their family.

'My mother-in-law died a thousand times that day. Only a mother can tell you how difficult it is to leave your child like that. In this case, it wasn't just a simple death. He had been attacked because of his religion. He could have been saved if he had been provided with proper medical care, but we had to leave him there. We had no choice. He was begging his mother to go. The lanes outside Trilokpuri were awash with blood and also littered with bodies, their limbs and hair hacked off. It was a tomb of corpses. Flies were already beginning to buzz around. I saw a young mother holding her baby and sitting in the doorway of her home. Behind her, the bodies of the men in her family were piled up.'

Darshan's mother-in-law collapsed as they exited Trilokpuri. She began hitting her head against the walls of nearby buildings and beating her chest with her hands. 'Darshan, everything is finished,' she cried. 'What will we do? Where will we go?'

'I held my mother-in-law's arm and said, "Mummy, we have to leave this place. We have to walk, otherwise they will kill the children too." I managed to convince her to walk with that threat of danger to her grandchildren. But Mummy was nothing more than a dead body that could walk. Her heart and soul never left Block 32.'

After walking for a few miles, Darshan and her mother-in-law reached the Patparganj Police Station, but the police officers present there refused to help them. 'A sub-inspector at the police station told us that he could arrange for food, but that he couldn't do anything beyond this as there were no orders. My kids were crying of hunger, they had not had any food since the previous day. So we agreed to the sub-inspector's offer and sat outside the police station, eating whatever little was given to us. Once we finished eating, the police officer requested us to leave. He said, "I'm sorry, my sisters, but I cannot do anything else. If anyone else gets to know about what I have done, I might lose my job."'

The sub-inspector told them to go to Pandav Nagar, but on their way, the women saw trucks piled high with dead bodies parked near the bridge over the Yamuna. They watched with horror as the bodies were flung into the waters below. 'We were too scared to go near that truck. We started running and ran for at least a few miles before we reached the Pandav Nagar Police Station. On reaching there, however, we were told to leave and go to a gurdwara in Pandav Nagar instead.'

The gurdwara was a partially constructed building. When Darshan and her mother-in-law finally got there, they saw groups of scared women collecting desecrated copies of the Guru Granth Sahib inside. 'On seeing the copies of the Guru Granth Sahib on the ground, a shock ran through my body, and for a moment I forgot about all my personal losses and started collecting its "Ang" (pages) instead.'

There were some seventy or eighty women inside the gurdwara. Most of them thought they would be safe there, but around midnight, that illusion was shattered when a group of men appeared, shouting loud slogans and trying to break down the main door. Roused from their sleep, the women rushed to the roof and began throwing stones and bricks down at the mob, which eventually dispersed. But the men didn't actually leave the site—they waited across the road menacingly for nearly five hours. They left only after shouting dire warnings to the women. Darshan told me, 'We were not scared when we heard them. By this time, we had nothing to lose. They had taken all that we had had, including our families.'

The women left the gurdwara the next morning. It was no longer safe, and there was a good chance that the mob would return. All of them walked to Damdama Sahib, which was almost eight miles away. After walking for almost two miles, they saw a group of military personnel and requested them for help. But the military personnel refused to help them and barred their way instead. The women were redirected to the Kalyanpuri Police Station, which meant that they would have to walk back. After over two days of walking fruitlessly across the city in search of safety and shelter, without any food or water for their children and themselves, the women were at their wits' end. Some of them stopped by the banks of the river to collect some water for the children. But the Yamuna's waters were brackish and muddy. 'I saw a mother giving her own urine to her children to drink. Others gave their children the dirty water that was flowing out of the drainpipes. That was the first time I understood the pain of my parents being refugees. Our condition was no different. We were a bunch of homeless women looking for water and safety. Women were crying inconsolably on the banks of the Yamuna. If the Yamuna could speak, she would testify to our horror. I saw women taking a bath in that water, and I also saw women trying to kill themselves in that same water.

'By the night of 3 November, most of us had lost all hope. Distraught women were insisting that they would not allow the mob to touch their daughters. They kept saying, "If they come, we will go with them, but not our daughters."'

When the women finally reached Kalyanpuri, they found foreigners there distributing water bottles and packets of biscuits to the victims who were straggling through the colony. 'Our own people were killing us, but these god-sent people on the road saw us and their tears didn't stop,' recalled Darshan.

From Kalyanpuri, the women were taken to the police station at Farash Bazaar, which resembled a refugee camp rather than a place of law and order. Once again, the women were left to their own devices. Only when Swami Agnivesh[4] arrived on the scene did things begin to change. He insisted that the police provide some safe space to the distraught families. Though initially hesitant, the police was forced to do his bidding, giving the families rooms in a newly constructed building next to the police station. Help slowly began trickling in from NGOs and civil society organizations, with the Nagrik Ekta Manch[5] being the first to arrive.

The Sikhs refused to take any help from political leaders. The Delhi Sikh Gurdwara Management Committee (DSGMC) provided them with relief materials and essentials. With the raw materials provided by the DSGMC, the Sikhs in the camp started a common kitchen. They were, however, living in sordid conditions. The state administration did not put up proper camps or provide any basic sanitation facilities. Toilets were flooding; there was no water in the camp.

Darshan Kaur told me, 'In the camps, when the police started the business of recording testimonies and FIRs, they did not listen to us or record anything that the Sikhs were telling them. They intimidated the widows and the old Sikh men. Their thumb impressions were forcibly taken and pressed on the copies of the FIRs.'

In almost every camp, all FIRs were filed in an omnibus fashion. Victims and survivors never got copies of the FIRs filed, nor were they aware of what had been recorded in these FIRs. Instead of registering separate FIRs for each complaint, the ones registered did not mention the names of the suspects and were vague in terms of details and information included. Prosecutions in these cases led to acquittals.

'There were many women in Trilokpuri who were raped, but they didn't talk about it for a reason we all know well. The society we live in is extremely cruel. Women often get blamed for the actions of others, especially men,' said Darshan.

Women who were raped during the 1984 violence did not speak of it, fearing a hostile public response. For many, it was linked to their family's honour as well. In some cases, it was the men in their families also stopped the women from filing cases, and in some, it was the mothers who did not report the rapes of their daughters, for the simple reason that nobody would want to marry into a house defiled by rape.

A woman I met during the course of my research in Tilak Vihar, introduced herself as *'Main chaurasi ki ladki hoon*. I am a girl of 1984.' She did not wish to be named. Instead, she told me, 'Call me a Kaur of 1984.'

When I asked about her family, she fell silent for a while. Then she said slowly, 'Nobody likes to be associated with us, their raped daughters and sisters, if we choose to speak about our traumas.'

She went on to add, 'Mothers tried to hide their daughters, mine also tried; she put a child in my lap and dishevelled my hair so that I would look older. But nothing helped. The men would come, discuss among themselves, choose a woman and then many like me were dragged off. Some were taken to the rooftops. Some were taken to half-burnt houses. Many were raped in the open, with other men surrounding them and watching what was happening like it was a live show. My mother and some other women tried to save me. But nothing deterred those monsters. I could see men forcing the women to leave our locality. I could see my mother standing there, from the roof where I was being raped. I began shouting, "Mummy, *mainu chaddke na jaayieen*. Mummy, don't leave me here." My mother didn't leave without me.'

It would take the intervention of the Indian Army for some of these young women to be able to return home. Many of them were rescued from the homes of their neighbours and from nearby villages like Chilla, in east Delhi. Yet, all of them stayed silent.

'In Trilokpuri, when women rushed out of their homes, men from the village of Chilla asked each other which one they fancied. Those women would then be kidnapped, and later, raped,' Darshan told me. In fact, according to Darshan, there was hardly any woman in her neighbourhood who was spared the indignity. Even nine-ten-year-old girls were raped. Darshan herself witnessed many rapes. The attackers would first empty the houses of men, burning them alive. Then, the women would be dragged inside the looted houses and gang raped. 'The unmarried girls will have to stay unmarried all their lives if they admit that they have been raped. No one would marry such a girl.' So, most women kept quiet. Today, most families do not openly acknowledge the fact that back then, they were worried that if they complained, the perpetrators would return to do the same things to their women again.

My first visit to Tilak Vihar, where families affected by the anti-Sikh pogrom were rehabilitated, was in December 2013, and I wasn't prepared for how overwhelming an experience it would turn out to be. There are hundreds of families living in this densely populated colony which is also colloquially known as Widows' Colony. While facing their own share of unique problems, most people here complain about the sordid conditions they have been living in. Yet, despite the poverty and the lack of sanitation, the one thing that stands out are their vivid accounts of losing loved ones in the massacres of 1984.

The first time I met Bhagi Kaur was at her home in Tilak Vihar. Widowed in the massacres of 1984, she is a mother of five, who lost ten other members of her family—apart from her husband—in the pogroms. We sat in her one-room home, but with three grandchildren also present in the same room, there was barely any space to move. I was direct and upfront about the nature of my visit, and I could sense that she did not really want me there. Small wonder. These were not comfortable conversations to have, neither for those who narrated their stories nor for those who listened. Nevertheless, I persisted.

When Bhagi Kaur began talking about the events of 1984, she was kind and generous with her memories, but she did not mince her words. 'When Indira Gandhi was murdered, all of us at Trilokpuri were saddened, but nobody expected that we would be so closely associated with the assassination,' she said. Bhagi Kaur's two sons, Balwant and Balbir, were aged two and five in 1984, and her daughters, Anita and Pinki, were two years and six-months-old, respectively. Along with her husband and family, Bhagi was quietly walking along a nullah on their way to the Kalyanpuri Police Station, when they were spied upon by the mob and attacked immediately. Bhagi Kaur's husband was bludgeoned to death. 'I had to leave my husband's body there. I walked to Kalyanpuri and at the police station there I saw a truck full of half-burnt bodies. I spent eight months in a camp living a penurious life.'

When I asked her if the government had helped them thus far, Bhagi replied, 'There is no meaning to any help unless the people responsible are punished. I'm sorry to say this, but nobody will understand what we are going through and no compensation can satisfy us.'

Today, amidst tears, Bhagi Kaur questions, 'Why was this written into my fate?'

In many of the stories that I heard, much like the story of Bhagi Kaur, the wounds remain as fresh and raw as they were thirty years ago. Every year, November takes these people back to 1984, trapping them in a hellish cycle of loss and grief.

Lakshmi Kaur, who has been living in Tilak Vihar for the past thirty years, was fifty-eight years old when I met her, but she looked much older. 'Stress has aged me,' she said. 'My husband was killed right in front of my eyes and we were looted of all that we had. Our boys' hair were cut off and our women were raped. They lit rubber tyres and threw them around our homes. Thirty years have passed since then, but I still panic sometimes.' Lakshmi's words testify to the suffering that the victims of the 1984 massacres have had to endure.

'Our families have been butchered,' she continued. 'We are still caged in the memories of 1984 while the people responsible are still free. Ask the women who had to jump over their family members' dead bodies in order to save themselves, ask them what they feel when they remember such incidents. No one came to empathize with us in our time of suffering and grief. All I ask is for some closure. Can anyone direct me towards my dead husband's ashes? Where are his remains? Was he buried or was he cremated? Am I not a citizen? Who will answer my questions?'

Lakshmi Kaur's questions reverberate across generations. The children of 1984 have grown up with trauma and violence being their first memories. With fathers and brothers lost to the killings, many of these children have had to abandon their studies and take on the roles of breadwinners. Indeed, the rate of school dropouts substantially increased in the aftermath of 1984, yet no official linkage has been made between the massacres and the number of children who dropped out. I filed an RTI seeking answers to these questions. I haven't received a response so far.

The year 1984 remains a shadow on the lives of even those who were not old enough to remember the killings. Those who were babies in the winter of 1984, for instance, confess to hazy feelings of loss—they don't remember their fathers. For their mothers, widowed in the pogrom, the insecurity and stigma of living in Widows' Colony in Tilak Vihar has never left.

Following the tragic aftermath of the 1984 anti-Sikh massacre, Sikh children became targets of relentless racial slurs and discrimination. In the wake of the community's profound loss, these innocent children endured the torment of derogatory remarks and hateful taunts hurled at them solely because of their Sikh identity. These scars of massacre were not just physical but also deeply psychological, as these children faced a hostile environment where their very existence was met with scorn and prejudice. Such targeted verbal abuse inflicted further pain on a community already grappling with the trauma of violence and loss.

Raja, thirty-five years old, told me, 'Everyone used to talk about their fathers in school. Other students used to call me Seekh Kebab. They would say, "He is from the fatherless Widows' Colony."'

These children, who are adults now, have lived with the perpetual fear that like their fathers, they too might be killed one day.

Surjeet Singh was seven years old in 1984. His mother dressed him in a frock and hid him inside their house in order to save his life. When I asked about his father, he started to sob. His father was killed in Sultanpuri, Block C. 'I have studied till Class

X, but I did not appear for the final matric examination. I was in depression throughout my schooldays. We never had enough money to support our education or even to buy books or uniform,' said Surjeet. His childhood was traumatic and filled with the memories of his father's brutal killing.

'People used to donate clothes and we used them as our uniform.' Surjeet was worried about the family's financial condition and to support his mother, he started working at the age of fourteen.

'The only thing I miss the most is the presence of my father in our lives. We have lived like orphans.' He remembers when they were at the Farash Bazaar Relief Camp, six to seven families were accommodated in those small rooms. 'Food was also not properly available for all of us. Discussing 1984 is like opening a painful wound,' he said.

'All of a sudden, our lives were ruined and our family setup became unstable. If you lose someone in your family, it shakes everyone. Imagine, I have seen my father being burnt alive.

'I was angry yet helpless. We are five siblings and our mother was the sole breadwinner in our family. Today, after thirty-two years, I am again helpless. I can't provide for my kids. I have spent half my life fighting against these odds and my memories of 1984. I am undereducated, but I am trying my best to make ends meet.'

The current generation of youth living in Tilak Vihar have inherited the scars and trauma of the anti-Sikh massacre. Nothing much has changed here.

In 2019, when I visited Tilak Vihar, it was the second day of the three-day prayers that are held annually for the victims of the carnage. Women and children of the locality gather near the Tilak Vihar gurdwara and prepare langar for everyone who visits. There is a photo museum in the gurdwara that the survivors of 1984 built in the memory of those killed in the massacre. This museum is a bridge between the young and the old, and it is the only way for a third generation to meet their relatives.

There were many different emotions on display when I visited the gurdwara. Some had tears streaming down their faces. Others had bowed their heads in tribute to the lost ones. In a bittersweet gesture, some of the younger generation were introducing their friends to photographs of their grandparents—people now gone but never forgotten.

8
From Pens to Guns

I met Darshan Kaur for the first time at her Rajaji Nagar home in Delhi, in 2016. I reached there around 7 p.m. with my colleague Sampurna Khasnabis. Darshan was waiting for us on the main road from where she took us into one of the congested lanes of the colony. Children were playing on the road in spite of the gathering darkness. Everyone seemed to know Darshan and we were stopped several times by neighbours wanting a casual, comforting chat. Darshan lived in a one-room flat which had an attached bathroom and a kitchen. She had done her best to make it a homely, cosy space. There was a single bed and a sofa set, and the walls were adorned with photographs of all the protests she had attended. The wall opposite her bed was an emptier one, with only a single garlanded photograph of a man on it. I asked Darshan whether this was her husband. Biting her nails, Darshan nodded.

Our conversation was difficult because of the depth and complexity of the emotions involved. Darshan found it hard to express what she had gone through in words and she broke down several times during the course of that first conversation. But one question that she asked me continued to reverberate throughout my research, and indeed, during the writing of the report on the subject, and now, finally, this book:

'Successive governments have advised us to forget the past and focus on the future. Put yourself in our shoes for a second. Is it possible to erase the bloody past?'

~

The hunting lodge of King Edward III, the ruler of England from 1327 CE to 1377 CE, is set in acres of lush green lawns in East Hampstead Park, in the county of Berkshire. It is built in the Jacobean style, and from the lawns, one can easily spot deer in the woodlands around or polo horses in the paddocks beyond. The lodge's history is as rich as its parks and woodlands. England's doomed Spanish queen, Catherine of Aragon, stayed here while she waited for King Henry's word on whether or not he would eventually divorce her in his pursuit of Anne Boleyn.

As Senior Campaigner, Youth and Activism, I had been invited to stay at the lodge, to review and draft the International Youth Strategy for Amnesty International.

In spite of its original ownership, the lodge had a well-documented history of the women of yesteryear—their experiences of infidelity and suffering; their displays of courage and strength. But could I, I wondered, say the same about the documentation of the suffering and courage of women in modern Indian history? In most cases, in modern India at least, the documentation of the bravery of women depended on the men in their lives. It is also true for similar instances around the world. My belief was further strengthened by a dossier of documents on the infamous massacres in Srebrenica in Bosnia that a friend of mine sent over to me via email. In July 1995, the Serbian army occupied the town of Srebrenica. Over the next five days, more than 8,000 Bosnian Muslims, or Bosniaks, mostly men and adolescent boys, were abused, tortured and killed in detention centres. Bosnia's Interior Ministry reported that during those three years of war, 50,000 women were raped and some were executed after being kidnapped. The genocide stands as one of the worst humanitarian disasters since the Second World War. Today, international organizations often ignore human rights violations against women even though very often, it is the women who are imprisoned, tortured and raped as retaliation for actions of their male contemporaries.

As I leafed through the dossier, I realized how similar the path of history and politics is across the world, and how easily women become the first casualty of every conflict, large or small. Rape and gendered segregation are common weapons of war and ethnic cleansing.

During the course of my research on the anti-Sikh massacres of 1984, the conversations that I had with the dozens of Sikh women I met—the Kaurs of 1984—led me to the realization that while these women were victims, they were also survivors. The consequences of their survival have been different for each one of them—some women took up arms while some remained

THE KAURS OF 1984

Nirpreet spent a restless night, unable to sleep and wracked with guilt, wondering if she had indeed chosen the right path for herself. But every time she thought of this, the rage in her mind rose up to overwhelm objectivity.

The atmosphere at Khalsa College was emotionally charged. Every now and then, news of fake encounters would come in which angered and alienated many young people in Punjab.

'Those were bloody days,' recalled Nirpreet. 'Everyday, young people were getting killed. We were angry and restless. Political leaders in Punjab had failed us. The Sikhs in Delhi had been butchered, but the prime minister was absolving everyone of their guilt. The butchers were given plum positions in the system. At that point, all logic failed us because of our simmering anger.'

Nirpreet then went on to describe the brutal murder of Harminder Singh, who was killed in 1986 at Nakodar in Jalandhar. 'They shot him at a sawmill belonging to Natha Singh. SHO (Station House Officer) Jaskirat Singh said to him that since you make speeches with this tongue, we will stop it today forever. He shot Harminder in the mouth with his revolver. That was a cold-blooded murder.'

Harminder's post-mortem was done in the dead of night on 4 February 1986 and his family was not allowed to witness his cremation.

In the tumultuous 1980s, Punjab found itself ensnared within the confines of a burgeoning police state, crying out for healing and reconciliation. Regrettably, the opportunity for such vital processes was forsaken, with the youth being cornered and marginalized instead. Across the global landscape, history offers little precedent for a nation's mature response when its citizens veer astray. Rarely has any state mustered the courage to declare, 'They are our people; we shall not resort to their destruction but shall endeavour to comprehend.' Alas, such sentiments, rooted in empathy and understanding, do not serve the insatiable appetite for political power acquisition. Fear, conversely, emerges as a potent instrument in this pursuit, a truth painfully evident in Punjab's narrative. Each passing day saw an escalation in the ruthless crackdown by law enforcement and governmental authority, resulting in the deaths of numerous young individuals. Amidst this atmosphere of fear and oppression, young people like Nirpreet found themselves irrevocably ensnared, trapped in the web of injustice and tyranny.

Nirpreet told me that she was chosen by the Khalistan Commando Force for a mission in Delhi because it was her city and she knew it well. She says she was an asset for the KCF because there were very few like her even in Punjab—she spoke good English, and was confident and friendly. She had helped the KCF on various other occasions before, renting homes for them in Jalandhar and arranging transport. In Delhi, her mission was to secure safe houses in the city for the militants. No one would doubt her because she was a student. Nirpreet believes that the KCF leaders trusted her with this mission because they knew she was angry and wanted to avenge her father's killing. In Nirpreet, the KCF had found someone they could blindly rely on.

'We planned to kill Sajjan Kumar, R.K. Dhawan and Rajiv Gandhi. I did not think twice about any consequences. I just wanted to avenge my father's killing and the harassment and intimidation that my family had faced.' For the assassination quiescent victims of state politics. There were women who hid inside the Golden Temple as the Indian Army stormed through. Others stood by their militant husbands, out of love and duty. Hundreds of them fell victim to bullets, to rape and to a collective loss of public and political memory.

I had read about the 1984 Sikh massacres and the horrifying, inhuman cruelties inflicted not just on the victims, but also on those who survived to tell their tales. I grew up in a Sikh household where we often discussed how our Gurus became martyrs for truth and justice and how the Sikhs fought against the mighty Mughals. To me, a child born six years after Operation Blue Star, the violence of 1984 and its actual meaning were remote realities. But it was all brought home to me during one of my family's trips to the Golden Temple, where, as my mother showed me the bullet holes in the wall, she began to sob. I couldn't believe that something like this could have happened to such a sacred place. That was, perhaps, the tipping point. From then on, I read and heard story after story about what had happened in the Golden Temple in 1984, about the combing operations the state launched to find Sikh militants, and the anti-Sikh massacres that ravaged Delhi in the aftermath of Indira Gandhi's assassination. There was then, as there is now, a deep sense of fear and insecurity. So many voices had been silenced during and after 1984. So many of these voices were those of women who had witness the insanity. What would happen now?

And so, on my second night in the hunting lodge at East Hampstead Park, I found that I couldn't sleep. My work had a mandate and a deadline, but there were so many stories yet to be told. While I knew that Amnesty International would not deny me the chance to dive deeper into this unexplored well of history, politics and emotions, I wouldn't have the time needed to do the research and then write. After all, the launch of the report I was already working on was now only a few weeks away.

At around four in the morning, I felt so restless that I went out onto the empty greens for a run. I was haunted by the memories of those whom I had already spoken to, by their tears and their stories. After nearly two hours of running in the freezing cold, I returned to the lodge and ordered a cup of coffee. I called my mother to tell her of my troubled thoughts.

'You're restless,' she said after hearing me out. 'You want to do something. Why don't you write about it?'

'I'm a man. Do you think I can justify their pain?'

'No, you can't,' said my mother. 'Believe me, no one can. But you can be their voice. You can be honest and take your readers through their journey. Finish your work for Amnesty and then tell me in detail about everything that happened to these women. I want to hear it from you. And,' she added, 'if you want to write about them, your gender should be the last thing that stops you.'

Her last words before she cut the call were, 'I love you. You're very strong. Don't let anything bother you.' That is when I decided that I would continue my research in order to try and bring these stories out from the shadows of history and time into the light of day.

Later that day, I had a presentation to give on how best to engage young people in the Global Amnesty Movement and increase their participation in the human rights movement. While I was presenting my slides to the audience, an email popped up on my laptop screen. It was from the office of the chief minister of Punjab, Prakash Singh Badal. Two days later, I flew back to

India to meet the chief minister and other political stakeholders in Punjab. I wanted to submit reparation plans for the victims of the 1984 anti-Sikh massacres. But even though I waited for Badal for over two hours at his official residence, I couldn't meet him. I ended up submitting the document to H.S. Bains, then political advisor to the chief minister.

That same evening, I had to meet Nirpreet Kaur, the victim of anti-Sikh violence who tragically lost her father in Raj Nagar, Delhi. A diminutive but fierce woman, she runs an orphanage in Chandigarh. Fourteen days after the anti-Sikh massacres, Nirpreet, along with her mother and her two younger brothers, boarded a bus to Punjab from the Kashmere Gate Bus Stand in Delhi. As would become evident over the course of our interactions, Nirpreet's story is one of a bright young Maths (Honours) student of Delhi University eventually taking up arms in order to seek revenge for her father's death.

It was a hot summer evening when I reached Nirpreet's home in Mohali. There was no electricity. It was dark inside the room, with only one half-burnt candle lit up in one corner. None of that, however, seemed to stop Nirpreet, who was sitting with a travel agent and planning an annual trip for the students at her orphanage. She looked up when I entered.

'Are you Sanam?' she asked.

'Yes.'

'Please, come in, welcome,' she said, gesturing to a seat. 'The power backup isn't working. Have a seat, and give me two minutes to finish planning this picnic.'

I could hear kids shouting and squabbling down the corridors. In between her discussion with the travel agent, Nirpreet would shout out to the kids, telling them to behave or nobody would get to watch television that night. Obviously daunted by this threat, the kids fell silent. Nirpreet looked at me and smiled. 'Sometimes, you have to use such tactics with kids.'

I smiled back, wondering if she had even noticed that it was rather dark inside the room. The annual picnic, to the Bhakra Nangal Dam that year, was fixed for the next week, and soon, the travel agent went his way. Asking her help to get some tea for us, Nirpreet left the room, only to return a few minutes later with a box of barfi.

'You're lucky that you're getting any,' she laughed. 'Otherwise I mostly see empty boxes!'

As we talked, it became obvious that Nirpreet was curious to know more about me before she began telling me anything. She asked me my full name and then enquired about my family history and other minute details. 'So, how long have you been working with the victims of 1984?'

'It's been almost two years,' I told her.

The conversation then drifted to the women of Widows' Colony in Tilak Vihar, where the wounds of 1984 are still fresh. As Nirpreet said, 'It is not just the women of 1984 but three generations of victims living there who have been failed by successive governments. I too, lost my faith in the justice system. After all, the same men who killed thousands were given party tickets to contest the elections by the Congress. Despite everything, Rajiv Gandhi won with a thumping majority. Days after the massacre, we were forgotten citizens. Today, three decades have gone by and we are still struggling to make ends meet.'

It does seem like the world has moved on, leaving these families still stuck in the pain from four decades ago. What they suffered in 1984 was catastrophic. But even now, after so many years, only a few people have come to terms with their loss. For the rest, little has changed.

Back in Nirpreet's home in Mohali, the candle in the corner began to sputter just as the electricity returned. I could see the room clearly now. The paint on the walls was faded, and the walls themselves were cluttered with an assortment of medals, trophies and newspaper cuttings. I asked Nirpreet about them and she said, 'Some have been won by the kids. The others were given to me by various organizations.'

Our conversation lapsed into silence for some time, and then Nirpreet began talking.

'After Papaji's death, we were broken as a family. There was obviously a huge financial loss, but the emotional loss was greater. Fear engulfed all of us. We were scared. His screams haunted me. I couldn't sleep for so many months. Whenever I tried to close my eyes, I could see images of the mob setting my father on fire over and over again.'

As I spent more time with her, it became clear that far from being victims of the militancy in Punjab, Nirpreet and many others like her were among the first women to pick up arms and seek revenge for what had been done to them in 1984. Their stories, I realized, would need to be told. The only problem was that there were far too many women. I would need to find a focus group to tell a cohesive story.

During one of our interviews, I asked Nirpreet if she could introduce me to some of the women who had been inside the

Golden Temple during Operation Blue Star. She told me that she would let me know in a few days, and so I wrapped up my field trip to Punjab and returned to Delhi. Personal calamity struck almost immediately with word of my father's illness reaching me on my arrival in Delhi. I rushed home to Jammu that same day.

A month later, my father passed away.

As it often does, life intervened and for the next two years, the stories that had captured my interest during my work with Amnesty had to be kept in abeyance. As I shuttled between Delhi and Jammu and tried to pick up the pieces left behind after my father's death, stories from my own family's personal history began to haunt me: how my paternal grandfather had fled from his palatial home in Muzaffarabad in 1947, hiding in forests with his brothers along the way to steer clear of mobs that had burnt down his house along with his four sons and wife during the Partition of India and Pakistan. Not all my family's stories are soaked in blood and fear, of course. My grandmother, married into an aristocratic family in what became Pakistan, lost her husband during Partition. All of twenty-one years old and a single mother to boot, she travelled two hundred miles from the newly formed Pakistan to Kashmir with her one-year-old son, to reunite with her brothers. These were the kind of stories that gave me both courage and hope.

In 2018, on Christmas Eve, almost two years later, I received a call from an unknown number. It was Nirpreet.

'If you're still researching 1984,' she said, 'come up to Chandigarh. We can have a detailed conversation about it.'

The very next evening, I boarded the Shatabadi Express train from New Delhi to Chandigarh. During the four hours it took to travel to Chandigarh, I thought about Nirpreet and all the other women like her, and how they had survived beyond fear.

I reached Chandigarh around 9 p.m. that night and called Nirpreet to fix a time for our meeting the next day. She asked me to come by around three in the afternoon. When I reached her home the next day, I found Nirpreet deep in discussion with a group of little girls. They hastily went inside upon seeing me, and Nirpreet asked her son to bring tea for both of us.

We chatted for a while about trivial things, until, without any preamble, Nirpreet said, 'My mother did not stay in Punjab for long. She thought my brothers would be influenced by the Sikh movement in Punjab and she wanted to keep her sons away. She wasn't worried about me.' She laughed a little and continued, 'Maybe she didn't know me well. Our society doesn't expect a woman to speak or be opinionated. They like women who obey orders and live a caged life.'

Then, she finally told me the rest of her story.

In July 1985, Nirpreet joined Khalsa College in Jalandhar to continue her studies. Back then, even a year after Operation Blue Star and the massacres that followed, Punjab was nothing less than a garrison. Paramilitary and armed forces were present at every nook and cranny of the city, and flag marches were a regular occurrence. Many school buildings were occupied by security forces. Policemen often appeared unobtrusively on campuses of educational institutes, dressed in plain clothes. Discreet inquiries were made about particular students, especially those involved with the All India Sikh Student Federation (AISSF). The Punjab of the mid 1980s was a police state, and it was no different from the accounts we hear of Kashmir today.

Nirpreet stayed with her uncle's family briefly before moving into the girls' hostel on campus. To her hesitant mother, Nirpreet explained that it was the best decision, since this allowed her to focus more on her studies. But it was while she was living in the hostel that Nirpreet began attending evening sessions organized by the AISSF. It wasn't long before she was a regular at these meetings, even speaking up on some issues.

'I was participating in all the college events to stop myself from thinking too much about Papaji's death, not that I was ready to forget or forgive, but staying busy helped.' Nirpreet's outspokenness at the AISSF meetings inevitably brought her to the attention of the federation's senior members. She was soon part of its inner circle and was given the task of convening meetings with other students. She was a good speaker, gaining the federation support among the student body. Her speeches were full of anger and grief, and it helped that many in her audience already knew of the tragic circumstances of her father's death. She became a mobilizer for the federation in due course, and was inducted into the women's wing of the AISSF in Khalsa College. During one of the functions of the federation, Nirpreet met Sikh youths who had picked up arms and were quite openly associated with the Khalistan movement. They also advocated armed insurgent fighting for the establishment of an independent Sikh homeland in Punjab. Soon, Nirpreet was part of the militancy that would ravage the state for over a decade after the massacres of 1984.

Nirpreet's actions are not surprising, in retrospect. Following Operation Blue Star, there were many young people who felt alienated in Punjab. Anger was brewing against the government, though its causes and motives were scattered. Nearly everyone wanted to avenge the death of a family member or the torture they had endured at the hands of the state. Many were enchanted by the idea of a separate homeland. As far as Nirpreet was concerned, she said, 'I found peace in Amritsar with the members of the AISSF.' Not just that, she also found her tribe amongst them.

Soon after her appointment as the president of the federation's women's wing in Jalandhar district, Nirpreet was introduced to the closed cabinet at Amritsar. As she started visiting the AISFF's headquarters more regularly, she began to get invited to all the top-secret internal meetings of the body. It was at one such meeting that she met Bimal Kaur Khalsa, her mentor.

Bimal Kaur was a nurse at Lady Hardinge Medical College in Delhi. Her husband, Beant Singh, had assassinated Indira Gandhi. She later became a member of Parliament from Ropar. In the early days, Nirpreet was very close to her and Harjinder Singh Jinda, a Sikh militant member of the Khalistan Commando Force (KCF), which was a Sikh militant organization.[1] Jinda was also one of the two assassins of Arun Vaidya, the chief of the Indian Army during Operation Blue Star.

As Nirpreet began to gain popularity, she was often followed by local newspapers and photographed. When one of her mother's cousins saw her photograph in the newspaper, he called Sampuran Kaur, Nirpreet's mother, directly. After speaking to her cousin, Sampuran called up Nirpreet at the hostel, asking if the reports were true. Was she indeed working for the Sikh movement? Was she organizing programmes for them?

'When Maa confronted me, I told her that I didn't know what she was talking about. I convinced her that like any other student, I was only attending the cultural programmes and debates organized by the college and that I had nothing to do with any political movement. I told her that my uncle and his family had never liked me. I said that they didn't want me to complete my studies. That's why, I said, they were putting up false allegations like this one.' Nirpreet laughed as she remembered the conversation with her mother. 'That's how I convinced my mother,' she continued. 'In fact, she became really angry with Mamaji!'

Sampuran Kaur rang up her brother almost instantly. 'She told him that he was trying to malign a fatherless daughter only because I had an opinion. She warned him not to do such a thing. She said that she had no issues with my participation in college events. In fact, she went one step further and said, "I also participated in the Akali Morcha. It is political, but it has nothing to do with secession."'

Years later, Nirpreet recalls her mother revealing that her uncle had scornfully retorted, 'Sampuran, she's making a fool out of you. I will give you proof next time. I don't wish ill on her or on you, but promise me that for Nirpreet's sake, you will come to Jalandhar whenever I call you. Both of you are family to me. I am worried for her.'

A few weeks later, a rally was organized in Dhilwan, in Kapurthala. Nirpreet's uncle saw an article about it in the local newspaper. He called Sampuran and insisted that she come to Jalandhar without telling her daughter. Sampuran agreed, boarding an early morning bus the next day. She went straight to her cousin's home and both of them decided to go to Nirpreet's college to find out if she was there or not. By then, of course, Nirpreet had already left the campus to attend the rally in Kapurthala.

She was thirteenth on the list of speakers at the rally.

Bimal Kaur was also there in Kapurthala. She wanted Nirpreet to come with her to Amritsar for a meeting with some senior members of the AISSF. So she asked the organizers of the rally to push Nirpreet up to number three on the list of speakers, right before Harminder Singh, the president of the AISSF in Jalandhar district.

When Nirpreet finished her speech and came backstage, she was told by one of the local members of the AISSF that Bimal Kaur had already left and that she should go to Amritsar for an urgent meeting. 'I was not carrying any change of clothes, so I told him that I would go back to my college first and then go to Amritsar.'

From Kapurthala, then, Nirpreet went back to Jalandhar with Harminder Singh on his scooter. On their way, she asked Harminder if he, too, was coming to Amritsar for the meeting, but he was not aware of any urgent meeting being scheduled at the federation's headquarters. He told her that he was going to meet the college principal in Jalandhar regarding the arrest of some students.

While Nirpreet was riding pillion on a scooter, her mother and uncle were having a heated argument with the hostel security guard because he had denied them entry. When the man didn't budge, they decided to go to the warden's house to ask his permission to enter the hostel. The warden, however, was not there, and they had to wait half an hour before he returned and granted them access.

But it was all in vain, for there was a lock on Nirpreet's hostel room door. She was clearly not there. In shock, Sampuran Kaur stood there, desperately wondering what would possibly happen next. She had managed to get her family away from the chaos in Delhi, only to land them all right into the storm in Punjab. Tears were rolling down her cheeks, but Sampuran Kaur forced herself to walk back down the stairs to tell her cousin that he had been right all along. Suddenly though, she spotted a group of girls walking her way. As they came closer, Sampuran Kaur recognized her daughter's face—Nirpreet was chatting with her friends, a glass of tea in her hands, and walking towards her mother.

When Nirpreet saw her mother, she was taken aback. 'Mummy? Mummy, what are you doing here? When did you arrive? Is everything okay?' she demanded. Sampuran Kaur, shaken and shocked, stood there speechlessly until Nirpreet hugged her and asked her again why she had come to Jalandhar.

'Can't I come here to meet you?' asked Sampuran tearfully. The two women hugged each other, but their thoughts were very different. Saying nothing of the relief she felt on seeing her daughter, Sampuran handed her a box of homemade sweets and asked her to come downstairs to meet her uncle.

'My mother asked me if I was happy living in the hostel or if I wanted to go back and live with my uncle and his family. But there was no way that I could have gone back. I was comfortable in my new life. It was liberating. So I told Maa that I got enough time to study at the hostel and that all my friends were there too. But I did ask for some money for new clothes. I wanted to attend the marriages of two of my seniors in Kapurthala. So my mamaji gave me the money. He asked me to visit him often and then both of them left.'

attempt, Nirpreet identified entry and exit points in Delhi and did a complete recce of the capital.

When she was assigned the operation, Nirpreet had one condition: that she would go to Delhi alone, and if a man was to go with her, he would first have to marry her. She was not, I found, worried about having to travel alone on a dangerous mission; rather, she was more fearful of being labelled a loose woman who was living alone with an unknown man. 'Two weeks before this, the wedding of one of my seniors, who was a friend and part of the AISSF, was called off when her future in-laws discovered her links with the Federation. I didn't want anyone to take my father's name and say that Nirmal Singh's daughter is staying with a man without being married to him. I didn't want to bring a bad name to my family's honour.'

For many of the Sikh women who survived 1984, there was no room for romantic imagination. Many joined the ranks of the militants only after the death of their fathers or brothers or because they were tired of police harassment.

Marriages among militants were not uncommon. It is a little-publicized aspect of militancy in Punjab. There were instances where women were forcibly married off to militants. Others chose to become Khalistani brides to escape the daily intimidation and harassment that they faced at the hands of security forces. There were, among these, a few who fell in love without thinking about the future. Nirpreet's was the latter case. For the militants, in turn, these marriages were a convenient method of camouflage and protection against police scrutiny. Additionally, the facade of a normal life provided them with a certain moral legitimacy in the eyes of the Sikh community.

Nirpreet clearly recalls the day when she first insisted on the marriage condition before the core team of the KCF during a meeting. The meeting was being held in a closed room with many members of the AISSF present, along with Bimal Kaur Khalsa, Baba Thakur Singh, a revered figure associated with Damdami Taksal, and Harjinder Singh Jinda.

Everyone in the room was shocked and angry when they heard her, everyone except Bimal Kaur who started laughing. Harjinder Singh Jinda asked, 'What strange demand is this?' But after a quick discussion among the core team, her demands were agreed to and Nirpreet was told that she would be given three choices and she would have to select one from among the men shortlisted.

A few days later, Bimal Kaur called Nirpreet to Amritsar and asked if she had made her choice so that the bridegroom could be called for the wedding. Nirpreet chose Roshan Lal Bairagi, a man originally from the Brahmanical Bairagi order who had converted to Sikhism and adopting the name of Gurdev Singh. Before marrying Nirpreet, Gurdev Singh had already begun his journey into militancy.

9
Militant Bride

In a twist of fate, on two separate occasions, even though the marriage between Nirpreet Kaur and Gurdev Singh was fixed, it couldn't take place on the scheduled days. On one occasion, it was Nirpreet herself who resisted because she did not want to get married in old clothes. The second time, things fell through because Nirpreet had to make a quick trip to Jalandhar from the AISSF headquarters in Amritsar in order to appear for her college exams. She left quietly at four in the morning without telling anyone. Her disappearance caused quite a panic at the AISSF headquarters, leading Bimal Kaur to send an AISSF volunteer in pursuit of her.

'I finished my paper at around three in the afternoon and when I came out of the examination hall, the guy that Bimal Kaur had sent was waiting outside for me. He told me to come with him as

Bimal Kaur had asked for me urgently. I took leave for eight days from the hostel and went back to Amritsar with the volunteer. When I met Bimal Kaur, she was quite angry and asked me if I was serious about the mission. When I saw how angry she was, I said that I couldn't have missed my exam, otherwise my mother would have found out about my involvement with the movement and I obviously didn't want that.'

Bimal Kaur then asked Nirpreet if she would like to be married the next day, but yet again, Nirpreet refused. 'I want to buy new clothes for the marriage,' she told her mentor.

The next day, both of them shopped for a few suits at Amritsar's famous Lawrence Road. Nirpreet's uncle, based in America, had sent her money for a transistor and a cycle. However, she chose to spend that gift money on the wedding accessories along with a few suits for Bimal Kaur as well. For a while, both women forgot about the reasons behind the wedding and about what lay ahead. 'Bimal Kaur and I were shopping without thinking about the mission. We were like any other women shopping for a wedding. We were discussing what dupattas to match and where to get the clothes dry-cleaned as most of them were silk suits. I was excited about the wedding and I didn't think about the fact that we might not even be alive after the operation or that we would be jailed. I was young and naïve.'

Nirpreet clearly remembers that on the day of her wedding, Harjinder Singh Jinda was very upset. 'He saw me excited about my marriage and he couldn't control his anger. He said, "What are you thinking? This is not Delhi, and this is not a normal wedding. There will be no baraat. Nirpreet, do you even realize that you are on a mission to avenge your father's death? We are arranging this wedding because you want it. You are getting married to a Kharku!'"

Harjinder Singh was calmed by Bimal Kaur, who told him, 'Let her do what she wants. After all, she is getting married.'

On the day of her wedding, Nirpreet got dressed in her new red suit and carried a purse in her hand. She had wanted a small engagement ceremony the day before, and she had insisted on a wedding photographer being present. Those photographs would later send her to Tihar Jail, but that day, she could never have dreamed of it. 'I was both nervous and excited.'

It was a small wedding held in the house of a movement sympathizer who had permanently installed the Guru Granth Sahib in one of the rooms in his home. Nirpreet did not inform her mother about the wedding. There was no one from her family who was present at the wedding, except for one of her relatives, Major Baldev Singh Ghumman, a Sikh militant.

'A man from the AISSF started the wedding proceedings by reading from the Guru Granth Sahib. My would-be husband was sitting next to me. Suddenly, all my nervousness and excitement vanished. I felt extremely scared and I began to get cold feet, but it was too late to back out. To regain my confidence, I thought of my father, and that helped. I would not shy away from what I was doing, even though I felt that in doing it, I was cheating my mother. But then, it was better surely to be a militant's wife than be his whore.'

Despite the ceremony, the atmosphere in the tiny room was tense as the couple took four rounds around the Guru Granth Sahib. The final prayer was interrupted by the sound of police sirens blaring outside. A few moments later, they heard someone loudly banging the front door of the house. The police had arrived. All the men inside the room rushed out, some through the rooftop and others through the backdoor, and escaped to their designated safe houses.

Bimal Kaur then went and opened the door, and the police barged in. They found only women inside the house, including Nirpreet. They demanded to know where the men were, and Bimal Kaur replied calmly that the men had gone to the railway station to drop off the groom's party. The daughter of the house, she gestured to Nirpreet, had gotten engaged that day. The police clearly didn't believe this story and they searched the house from top to bottom. They found nothing and left shortly. After they had gone, Bimal Kaur told the women gathered in the room that the house was no longer safe for them. The next day, they went underground.

Twelve days after her wedding, the Delhi Police picked up Nirpreet's husband. He was never heard of again. Nirpreet, then pregnant with her son, went back to Delhi and showed her wedding pictures to Sampuran Kaur and told her that she was engaged. 'I just told her I was engaged. I didn't want to tell her that I was already married. She would have been not just disappointed, but heartbroken.' Despite this small act of consideration, Sampuran was furious. She commanded her daughter to tell her everything. But in the end, as Nirpreet says, 'My mother had no choice but to accept whatever I said.'

Soon after this, the Delhi Police knocked on their door too and the house was searched. The wedding photographs that Nirpreet had insisted upon taking were seized. If those photographs had never existed, nobody would have known that she was married to Roshan Lal Bairagi.

Nirpreet was arrested from her mother's home and taken into police custody for questioning. She claims that her photographs were leaked to the police by someone within their circle and that this person had told the police everything about her wedding and had also given the police the address of her mother's home.

As it turned out, Nirpreet's husband was also being held in the same police station. He had managed to sneak in $5,000, which he gave to the police officer on duty in exchange for Nirpreet's release. The bribe worked and Nirpreet was given free passage. Roshan Lal asked her to tell everyone that he had been arrested. She did so immediately upon escaping in a hired taxi. She warned everyone of Roshan's arrest and told them that it would be best to go underground and dispose off their weapons as well. The tip worked. Nobody else was arrested.

It was, however, too late for Nirpreet to hide the fact of her marriage any longer. That night, she went back home and confessed everything to her mother. Sampuran Kaur was outraged and furious but there was obviously nothing that she could do. She had no words of advice for her daughter, but she was terrified for her safety. 'What have you done, Nirpreet? They will kill him, and they won't spare you either.'

Nirpreet recalls being absolutely numb in the face of her mother's anger and despair. Instead, all she could ask her mother was if it would be proper to contact Roshan Lal's family and let them know about what had happened. 'If you have their contact details then, of course, you must,' Sampuran said irritably. Roshan Lal's family lived in Amritsar and Nirpreet decided to travel personally to Amritsar to tell them of his arrest. She lay low in Delhi for a day or so before leaving, but in spite of the precautions she took, the news of her sensational arrest was all over the newspapers the next day.

It was perhaps a coincidence that the day she arrived at the AISSF headquarters was also when Roshan's worried father was there to ask if anyone knew anything about his son's whereabouts. Daughter-in-law and father-in-law met at the AISSF headquarters for the first time, as strangers. It was plain that Roshan Lal had never told his father about his marriage.

In Punjab, she again sought refuge with AISSF and delivered her son in Ludhiana. By then, she was already a proclaimed offender in Delhi. It became increasingly unsafe for her to stay in one place. 'I was on the run from December 1986 to May 1988, hiding in the homes of Khalistani supporters across India,' she recounted.

In December 1986, Nirpreet's mother was sentenced to three years in Delhi's high-security Tihar Jail for sheltering a terrorist. 'She didn't even have a clue about what I was up to,' said Nirpreet.

In May 1988, the Punjab Police and paramilitary forces launched Operation Black Thunder against armed militants who had built up a fortified stronghold within the Golden Temple in Amritsar. Forty extremists were killed and several others were arrested. Nirpreet was also amongst those hiding inside the Golden Temple when she was arrested. Before that, even though she was on the run for two years, she had continued to work underground for different outfits. Finally, upon her arrest, she was lodged in jails in Punjab before being shifting to Tihar Jail in New Delhi.

During her time in police custody, Nirpreet was tortured, harassed, called all kinds of humiliating names and always interrogated in the absence of a female police officer, which is in itself an illegal act. Meanwhile, Sampuran Kaur hadn't heard of her daughter for over a year, until she was brought to Tihar Jail. Only then did Sampuran discover that Nirpreet was alive. Since they were lodged in the same jail, mother and daughter both pleaded with the jail's wardens to allow them to meet. The request was eventually granted. As soon as the iron gates of the cell were unlocked, Sampuran rushed to her daughter, weeping. It was the first time she had ever been away from her daughter for so long, and it was also the first time she was meeting her grandson.

'After spending time in jail, I just wanted to live with my family and do something for my mother. But there was continuous social pressure on me to get married again. I wasn't interested, but eventually, I succumbed under all the pressure. On 21 September 1997, I got married again, this time to an NRI travel agent who also ran an import-export business. He had previously been a Khalistani sympathizer.'

Nirpreet's second husband's family was not in favour of their marriage. She was not welcome in their house. So she rebuilt her new life in Delhi and started living with her husband in Tilak Nagar. She also began visiting Tilak Vihar to help the widows of 1984, but her husband did not approve of this. He would often stop her from visiting Tilak Vihar, afraid that her visits might rekindle old militant connections. Nirpreet gave up her visits, but secretly, she continued to extend financial support to the bereft families.

After two years of marriage, Nirpreet got pregnant again. There were extended periods of separation from her husband during this phase in her life as he began spending long stretches of time outside Delhi. When her second child, also a boy, was born, her mother-in-law came to visit them and she invited Nirpreet to accompany her back home to Hoshiarpur. Nirpreet agreed to the proposal, but when she reached Hoshiarpur, her son was taken away from her. She was told that he would be better off with his grandmother. Nirpreet was even prevented from feeding her son. 'I don't want our grandson to be fed by a terrorist,' her mother-in-law said to her. 'I know what kind of a woman you are. You will destroy our home and my son's life.'

Nirpreet stayed quiet in the face of this verbal abuse.

'I was quiet because I wanted to live with them and give my children a normal childhood away from the shadows of my past. But sometimes I felt that staying in the Khalistan movement would have been better than this domesticated life. At least, there I was equal and commanded some respect.'

Eventually, Nirpreet returned to Delhi, this time suffering from a severe case of depression. Her son had been taken away from her and her husband refused to listen to her pleas that the child be returned to her.

Nirpreet told me that after her testimony against Congress leader Sajjan Kumar, she was approached by H.S. Hanspal, a member of the National Commission for Minorities, to reach a compromise with Sajjan Kumar. She was also approached by Sajjan Kumar's men, who offered her Rs 3 crore along with a flat and a car for keeping his name out of the court case. She declined all of these offers. Sajjan Kumar[2] continues to deny all allegations against him, despite evidence suggesting otherwise.

I asked Nirpreet if she regrets her decision to pick up arms.

'Not for a single day have I ever regretted picking up arms,' she said. 'It was the right decision and it was the need of the hour. The government created a suffocating environment. Picking up arms was more liberating.'

10
The Daughter of a Cop

In the aftermath of my father's death, I had shelved the idea of doing this book, despite having already penned half of its draft. But in December 2019, fate stepped back into the picture with Nirpreet calling me out of the blue. She wanted Vrinda Grover's[1] telephone number. On an impulse, I asked her if she might be able to arrange for me to interview some women who had taken up arms after 1984. Nirpreet said she could, because, as luck would have it, one of her friends who had been involved in the movement was back in the country. She could arrange a first meeting.

I travelled to Chandigarh the very next day, reaching the city at around 5.30 p.m. I called Nirpreet to fix a time for our meeting, but she was on her way out of the city. She would only be back next week. I had, quite unexpectedly, a lot of time to kill, so I took out my diaries and began skimming through my notes.

Suddenly, a line in one of my diaries jumped out at me: *Look for Satnam Singh Chinna's wife.*

That's exactly what I did. After dinner, I began researching Satnam Singh Chinna. A Sikh militant, Chinna had been the leader of the Bhindranwale Tiger Force of Khalistan.[2] I found a video on a streaming platform about his role in the Khalistani movement along with some superficial information on his family—his wife and two sons, who were right there in Chandigarh. I made note of the information and sent it to my journalist friends in Chandigarh. Nobody, however, seemed to know anything at all.

I went back to the drawing board and called some friends at the offices of PTC[3] Punjabi. Again, I met with nothing. This time, I felt the onset of panic. An entire Saturday had somehow passed and I hadn't managed to either interview Nirpreet's sources or find Satnam Singh Chinna's wife.

I was left with just one more day in Chandigarh and I had no idea how or where to start.

In the evening, a friend from Punjab University called me to check how things were going. I told him of my frustration over finding no leads on Satnam Singh Chinna's wife. 'Why don't you speak to some lawyers?' he asked. 'You know so many of them in Chandigarh. Maybe someone has represented her or knows her through the lawyers' network?' It sounded like a good plan to me, so I went ahead and drafted a text message to my friends who were either lawyers themselves or who knew social activists and lawyers in the city.

By the next morning, I had six different telephone numbers, out of which five were not working and one was switched off. I had some hopes of eventually getting through the switched off number, so I kept trying.

Around two in the afternoon, I got a call from an unknown number. When I picked up the phone, a woman said politely, 'My missed calls alert is showing that I received twenty calls on my phone from this number. Who is it?'

I told her my name and the reason why was I calling. Then, I asked her name.

She said, 'I am Jasmeet Kaur.'

I casually inquired if she knew Satnam Chinna or if she could provide me with his wife's contact information. Without missing a beat, she responded, 'I am Jasmeet Kaur Chinna, Satnam's wife. How can I help you?' The revelation caught me off-guard—it was a stroke of pure luck.

We spoke for about fifteen minutes. I told her about my research and asked if we could meet. She agreed, but then added, 'I am at my friend's place in Mohali. Please come by 3 p.m. if you can and don't be late. I have to do some washing and also cook the evening meal.'

She sent me an address that was close to the Mohali Cricket Stadium. I called my friend from Punjab University and he immediately volunteered to come along with me.

When the two of us reached the house, however, we met with a slight setback. A clean-shaven man answered the door in response to our ringing the bell. He told us that nobody was at home and then asked us to leave. When I insisted that Mrs Chinna had called us to meet her at this address, the man got a little belligerent. It was clear that the man wouldn't budge, so we came back outside and I called Jasmeet Kaur on her phone. She came out almost immediately, apologizing profusely for the behaviour of the man and ushering us into the house. Though she must have been in her mid-fifties, Jasmeet Kaur looked very young.

'*Je aaya nu.* Welcome,' she said, greeting us in Punjabi.

Once inside, I realized that the house looked very familiar, almost as if I had been there before. Could it be the same house where I had met and interviewed Nirpreet a few years ago? Though the room we were in was well-lit and its walls freshly painted, it still looked the same.

Jasmeet then told us that Nirpreet had gone to Gurdaspur for some personal work. 'She never leaves her home empty, so she asked me to stay here while she was away.'

During the course of my explaining more fully what I was doing in Chandigarh, it became evident that it was Jasmeet who Nirpreet had been talking about when she'd said that one of her friends who was part of the movement was back in the country. It was a really lucky coincidence.

Nothing in Punjab, however, starts without the offering of food, and before we could begin our conversation, Jasmeet brought out some tea and homemade biscuits.

'It is going to be a long conversation,' she said, 'and I don't want you to fall asleep!'

Once we were settled with the hot steel glasses of tea in our hands, she sat quietly for a moment before beginning to talk, 'Oh, Sanam! Those were the toughest days. Nothing seemed normal. People were getting killed and the torture of innocent people in the hands of Punjab Police was not unknown. The regime was also becoming more and more brutal with every passing day. Where should I start? So much has happened over the years and it just doesn't end.'

Jasmeet was born in Kandial, Batala. She had three brothers and a sister. Her father was an inspector in the CID in 1984. Back then, he had been posted at Amritsar but maintained residence in Ajnala, a town near Amritsar. Jasmeet was pursuing a master's degree in English at Khalsa College when Operation Blue Star was launched. Teary-eyed, but smiling, Jasmeet continued with her story.

'My father unknowingly played a key role in my decision to join the movement. He was influenced by the Dharam Yudh Morcha and encouraged all of us at home to participate in it. But I think it wasn't just him; every Sikh in Punjab was involved. His name was Dalbir Singh Randhawa. I also felt that the atmosphere was very positive. People were getting close to their religion; even the clean-shaven men had started keeping beards. The atmosphere in Punjab was very different in those days. The state was heavily militarized. Even the colleges were not spared.'

At Khalsa College, Jasmeet was influenced by her senior Upkar Kaur. She considered Upkar to be her mentor. Jasmeet recalled that it was Upkar who taught her how to read religious scriptures and who introduced her to the realities of the Khalistan movement. Before long, Jasmeet was a regular at the protests taking place across the city, even courting arrest several times long before Operation Blue Star.

'Once, a protest march was taken out for Ranjeet Singh who had been jailed for killing the leader of the Nirankari Mission.[4] We were so naïve. We blindly followed Upkar during the march—a group of thirty odd girls, carrying Indira Gandhi's effigy, and we had to take it to the city square. Upkar also gave us the script for the protest slogans.'

Upkar Kaur told the girls that first, she would shout, 'Ranjeet Singh!' The girls had to respond with 'Release him!' Next, she would say, 'Killers of Sikhs!' This had to be answered with 'Punish them!'

'It sounds funny to say this now, but we messed it all up when the time came. It was the first protest for most of us and we were confused. None of us had done this before, and certainly not with the media present. So when Upkar shouted, "Ranjeet Singh," we shouted "Punish him," instead of "Release him!" She was so angry. She shouted at us and told us to get it right. So we tried again. This time, she shouted "Killers of Sikhs!" We shouted, "Release them!" It was embarrassing, but it happened because she changed the sequence.'

But when news of the attack on the Akal Takht Sahib in June 1984 spread, humour was forgotten. Everyone was terribly upset and angry as word flew around of the desecration of the temporal seat of the Sikhs. Months after Operation Blue Star, Jasmeet started experiencing mood swings and stopped talking to everyone. 'Nobody cared about mental health in those days. I was depressed. I stopped going to college and did not appear in my exams.'

Then came the news of Upkar Kaur's death. One of the few openly armed women militants of her time, Upkar was at the Akal Rest House when she was killed. In fact, Jasmeet's father had even seen Upkar's dead body. The news tipped Jasmeet over the edge. She stopped talking to her family and stopped eating as well. She fell sick. Her family even worried that she was possessed. They took her to different god-men in and around Amritsar. During this time, Jasmeet turned to religion almost fanatically and became a regular at the Golden Temple.

In 1986, Jasmeet met Nirpreet Kaur, with whom she would eventually become good friends. She also met and befriended former militant Karaj Singh Thande.

Thande, once a promising weightlifter in the Mahar regiment where he held the position of a sepoy, transitioned into a self-styled lieutenant-general of the Khalistan Liberation Force[5] by 1985.

Karaj Singh Thande was close to Jasmeet's father. He used to call him Mamaji. Jasmeet's interaction with him increased when he started visiting her house and she ended up meeting a lot of people in the Khalistan movement through Karaj Singh.

Soon after Operation Blue Star, however, Jasmeet's father asked her not to go to the Golden Temple. She angrily snapped back at him, 'It was you, Papa, who asked us to join the Dharam Yudh Morcha. I can't stop going to the Golden Temple. Now is the time to take revenge for what they have done to us and our places of worship, and you are asking me to forget everything and stay at home.'

Dalbir then told his daughter that he was worried for her safety. He had heard of informants among the ranks of the Khalistani movement. 'I asked him how he knew this and he said that he had recruited a woman to tell him what was happening inside the Golden Temple.' Jasmeet pressed her father for more information, but he refused to tell her anything further. All he wanted was her assurance that she would not go to the Golden Temple any longer. 'He told me that I wouldn't even be able to recognize these people. They were in reht maryada[6] and I wouldn't be able to tell the difference.'

Next day, in a meeting at the Golden Temple complex, Jasmeet brought this up for discussion. She narrated everything her father had told her, but nobody believed her. Instead, it was alleged that it was she who might be the mole in the complex, particularly since her father was a CID officer. 'This broke my heart. It was because of this that I stopped going to the Golden Temple.'

A few days later, Jasmeet received a cautionary message from Nirpreet. If Jasmeet were to revisit the Temple, she would face grave danger, with her life at risk and her body possibly disposed of in a gutter. When I inquired about who threatened Jasmeet, she responded, 'The threat came from someone prominent during the militant movement.' However, she declined to provide any additional information. Jasmeet felt she had nobody to confide in, as those who could have supported her were absent. Karaj Thande was in Pakistan, but Amarjeet Singh, another Khalistani supporter, was in Chandigarh, and he regarded Jasmeet as his sister. He assured her that nothing would happen and that no harm would come to her. He would personally ensure it.

'He asked Nirpreet to tell me to come to the Golden Temple without any fear. I was also determined to go to the Golden Temple and identify all the informers. I let out a message to the man who had sent me the death threats, *'Apni gali main kutta bhi sher hota hai.* Even a dog thinks of himself as a lion in his own area. Come out and I will see you. I wasn't scared of them.'

But despite her bravado, after this incident, Jasmeet stayed away from the Golden Temple. She stopped talking to her friends.

She also tried to take her own life, so deeply upset was she by the allegation that she might be the mole. 'I suddenly started hating all my friends in the movement. I was there because I believed in the cause. I wanted to support the movement. I did not have any other agenda.'

A few weeks after her suicide attempt, Jasmeet decided to return to mainstream life. She cut her hair and her ties with the Khalistani movement. She resumed her studies again. 'I started going to the cinema and went shopping and eating with friends in Amritsar.'

Yet, there was an odd push and pull of emotions that persisted. Whenever there was news of a seizure of arms from khadkus, or of an encounter with the police, it would upset Jasmeet. When Karaj Thande returned from Pakistan, he asked Jasmeet to meet him, but she refused to go. She sent word to him via a messenger that there was no point in reaching out to her for she had left the movement behind.

In 1988, the Sikh militant movement entered Jasmeet's life yet again. After Operation Black Thunder 2,[7] Dalbir Singh Randhawa was transferred from Amritsar. It was in Amritsar that Jasmeet met Ranjeet Singh, a friend of her uncle and an opium smuggler. He was also related to Resham Singh Chinna, an absconding militant.

Ranjeet Singh was a frequent guest at Jasmeet's house where he sought her father's help in getting his family members released from the police custody. Her father had helped Satnam Singh Chinna's family on three previous occasions as well. Jasmeet recalled an incident when Ranjeet came to their house and asked Dalbir to help them teach Leftist activist Hardev Singh a lesson.

Ranjeet said, 'Hardev was an alcoholic who regularly molested women under the influence. But he was also a local politician with immense clout.' Dalbir said he couldn't intervene on the matter.

While Dalbir was away, Ranjeet visited their house yet again. This time, he spoke to Jasmeet. 'He told me that Hardev Singh was a womanizer who misbehaved with every woman in the village Chinna. No one could touch him because of his political connections. They wanted to teach him a lesson.' In reality, however, Satnam and his men wanted to do more than that. Satnam, as Jasmeet would discover later, wanted to murder Hardev Singh. Ranjeet told Jasmeet that Hardev Singh was from Satnam's village and Satnam was regularly mocked by his neighbours for his inability to make Hardev Singh pay for his actions. 'If you can't protect the women of your own village,' he would be asked, 'then what can you do?' Ranjeet asked Jasmeet if she could get Hardev Singh alone out of the village. 'I thought that a man like Hardev Singh, who has no regard for women, must be taught a lesson. Moreover, it looked like a simple enough task. So I immediately agreed to help them,' said Jasmeet.

Ranjeet told Jasmeet that before she actually carried out the mission, he would arrange a meeting between her and Satnam Singh Chinna and only if the latter approved, would she go ahead with the mission. 'Ranjeet warned me that no one should know about my meeting with Satnam and about the plan to trap Hardev Singh.'

Jasmeet's meeting with Satnam Singh Chinna took place in a nondescript village near Amritsar. She reached the pre-decided location on time on her motorbike. It was an abandoned home in the middle of fields that were guarded by Satnam's men.

Jasmeet was asked to sit in a pitch-dark room, which was sparsely furnished with only one chair and the bare frame of a bed. Suddenly, the door opened and Satnam Singh Chinna entered the room. He walked in with his back to Jasmeet, clearly to hide his identity. The exchange that followed between the two was short and crisp.

'Will you do this job?' Satnam asked.

'Yes, I will,' responded Jasmeet.

'How much money will it take and how will you do it?'

'Not more than Rs 5,000. Ranjeet has told me that Hardev Singh is a womanizer, so I will honey trap him and lure him out.'

'You bring him to us and we will take care of the rest,' commanded Satnam Singh, and with that the conversation was over.

Next day, as per the plan, Jasmeet left home early for Chinna village to meet Hardev Singh. She was dressed in a pair of jeans and her hair was cut short—the perfect disguise to fool anyone into thinking that she was not a local girl.

'I took my motorbike and went to the village. I saw the same men in the village whom I had seen the day before guarding the house where I had met Satnam. They were there to help me. Hardev Singh was going to his fields to open the water supply. I was alerted about his movements by two men who were keeping an eye on him. While Hardev Singh was returning from his field, I stood there on the road and acted like my motorbike wasn't working. One of Satnam's men also walked over to where I was standing and pretended to check my motorbike. When we saw Hardev approaching us, Satnam's man declared loudly that he couldn't fix the motorbike.'

When Hardev Singh came closer, Jasmeet asked him for help. Introducing himself, Hardev agreed and asked where she had come from. 'I told him that I was a journalist from Delhi and that I was visiting Punjab to interview people who had been attacked by militants.' Hardev then told Jasmeet that he was also a victim of the militancy in Punjab. Perhaps, he suggested, she would like to know his story? 'I told him I didn't have the time that day, but that I could interview him some other time.'

Hardev helped fixing Jasmeet her motorbike and they fixed a time to meet up the day after, and Hardev Singh told Jasmeet that he would wait for her at the village bus stop.

Jasmeet left after that. She had to inform Satnam's team that a meeting had been fixed. They had agreed earlier that Satnam's team would wait outside the Raja Sansi Airport in Amritsar and Jasmeet would pass by through the airport after seeing Hardev Singh. If she blew the horn of her motorbike, it meant the meeting was confirmed. If she didn't, it meant that she would try again.

'A day after, I went to the village to meet Hardev. He picked me up from the bus stop and took me to his home, where he offered me some boiled eggs. I am a vegetarian, so I refused, saying that I fasted every Tuesday. So he gave me some milk to drink instead, and then began telling me how he had been attacked by militants. Over the next few days, we met every day. When I was confident that he had finally begun to have feelings for me, I informed Satnam's team through Ranjeet.'

Satnam was pleased. He instructed Jasmeet to get Hardev out of the village, without his usual security entourage. 'Hardev agreed to meet me alone, but when he turned up at the rendezvous point, he had his gunmen with him. I pretended to be annoyed with him.

Then I lied and said that I had wanted to be alone with him, but since that was now impossible, there was no point in my staying there and I would much rather go back.'

Hardev fell for the bait. Excitedly, he asked his security men to leave.

'We got into a taxi and I asked Hardev Singh to sit next to me. We drove into the interiors of the jungle outside the village. Soon enough, we were being followed by a car, but Hardev didn't notice, and by the time he did pay attention to the car, it was too late.'

Overpowered easily by Satnam and his men, Hardev Singh was taken away in the car. From that point onwards, Jasmeet says she doesn't know what happened, but her involvement in the entire affair is a telling insight into how deeply the young Sikh women of 1984 were embroiled in local and regional politics, no matter how gruesome things were.

It wasn't long after his murder that Jasmeet was picked up by the local police. Hardev Singh's security men had informed them that they had last seen their master driving away in a taxi with a young woman—a journalist from Delhi, with short hair and in a pair of jeans. She had, they said, often taken local taxis. On questioning the taxi drivers of Amritsar, the police gathered enough information to put together a sketch of Jasmeet. One of the drivers also informed the police that the so-called journalist had been looking for a rented accommodation and had met some local property dealers as well. It didn't take the police too much time after this to arrest Jasmeet. It was 1990 and her father was the deputy superintendent of police (DSP) of Ferozepur.

While in police custody, Jasmeet says that she was tortured. 'They used to beat me with rubber belts. I told the police about the vehicle in which Satnam's men had taken Hardev Singh, and they found it. Then I told them that I knew nothing beyond this.'

In that meeting I remained unconvinced that Jasmeet was unaware of what had transpired with Hardev at the hands of Satnam and his men. It seemed she was intentionally keeping this knowledge hidden from me, at least for the time being.

Some argue that Hardev Singh, who had previously worked for the army, was a communist activist and he was killed because he disagreed with the extremists and preached an anti-sectarian message. His head was cut off and placed at the entrance of the Chinna village. Hardev Singh was not the only communist activist killed during the militancy period in Punjab; there were others as well.

Jasmeet's father sent her a message via one of his colleagues, asking her to not say a word beyond what she had already told the police. He warned her to not change her testimony or else she would be repeatedly tortured for more information. Then he came to meet his daughter, but she asked him not to come back to the jail again. She didn't want him associated with her. 'My father was the only source of bread and butter at home, I was worried for his job. That's why I didn't want him to get into trouble because of me. Though when my father met me at the police station unofficially, he told me he was proud of my actions.'

It was in jail that Jasmeet met Nirpreet Kaur again; the latter had been arrested during Operation Black Thunder. Jasmeet couldn't help but chuckle as she recounted the unlikely friendships forged within those stark walls of jail. She and Nirpreet, among the handful of inmates fluent in English, found themselves drawn to a woman from Africa. In a curious exchange of languages, they taught the African woman snippets of Punjabi, bridging cultural divides in the most unexpected settings. Their days became a mosaic of shared conversations and camaraderie as they navigated the monotony of prison life together.

Once she was released on bail after a year, Jasmeet decided not to return home, and instead, devote herself fully to the Khalistan movement. She had already spent more time in jail than what she thought she deserved. She went to Ferozepur first to meet her father, who was ill and admitted in a hospital. He pleaded with her to not return to the movement, but Jasmeet told him sadly that it was too late.

During one of her court visits, Jasmeet met Satnam's cousin who told her that Satnam was thankful to her. He wanted to meet her. While Jasmeet had been in jail, Satnam had taken care of all her expenses. In fact, even her bail bonds had been paid by him. Now, together with his cousin, Jasmeet travelled to then Uttar Pradesh, now Uttarakhand, where Satnam was hiding out in the dense forests of the Terai. A day after she arrived in UP, Satnam came to see her. With him were twelve men in two jeeps. 'At that moment, I felt that I was truly part of something bigger and more important than myself,' said Jasmeet.

When he saw her, Satnam expressed his gratitude and said, 'Thank you very much. We are grateful to you. Now tell us, what can we do? What's your plan?'

While Satnam was talking to Jasmeet, she couldn't see his face properly. Answering his question, she said, 'Whatever I have done so far, I have done out of my own personal convictions; it has all been for a cause I believe in.'

Satnam then asked if they could do anything to make her life better. In response, Jasmeet said that she wanted to be a part of the movement, but no longer as someone who carried messages. 'I told him that I wanted to fight.' Satnam seemed understandably shaken. 'You are an educated young woman,' he said. 'Take five lakh rupees from us and go back home or leave this country. Get married and start a new life abroad or somewhere else.'

Jasmeet retorted, 'I never did this for money.'

'We are helpless,' Satnam replied. 'We don't allow unmarried girls in the movement. If you really want to stay with us, there are twelve men here right now, choose anyone and marry him. Then you can stay with us.' He went on to suggest his uncle's son, also a graduate, as a likely candidate for Jasmeet.

'I had never thought of doing something like that, and I did not want to marry or have kids while being a part of the movement.' Jasmeet asked Satnam for some time to think, to which Satnam agreed, saying, 'I will come back after three days. You have until then to decide.'

Jasmeet recounted that over the next couple of days, she thought long and hard about the matter and decided that if marriage was the only way for her to join the movement, then why not marry Satnam himself?

On the third day, Satnam returned in the evening with his entourage. For the first time, he stood before Jasmeet with a lamp raised to his face so that she could finally see him clearly. 'He asked me if I had decided who I was going to marry. My voice was shaking as I told him that if marriage was the only way out, then I would marry him only.' In the silence that followed, Jasmeet waited nervously for his reaction.

When Satnam finally spoke up, all he said was, 'I have to speak to the others in my team and we will decide together.' He then asked Jasmeet to sit with him in the Jeep that he was driving. 'Someone told us not to go via the main road as the police had set up a Police nakka, check point, there. So we took an interior route. Satnam drove very rashly that night and we met with an accident. He was hurt badly and even broke his rib. I also had a few injuries.'

Satnam managed to somehow drop Jasmeet to Gurdwara Shri Nanakmatta in Rudrapur, Uttarakhand, and told her that he would be back soon. The caretaker at the gurdwara was known to Satnam and he arranged for Jasmeet's stay.

Jasmeet was there for six days, and during this entire period, she had no contact with Satnam and no information either about him or his men. As the days passed, she grew angry and thought that Satnam and his team had reneged on their promises to her, and that no one would come back for her. After the Hardev Singh case, she had become a known face in the militant circles in Punjab, and while she was waiting for Satnam, she was approached by other militant outfits, all of them asking her to join them. She maintains to this day that she no longer wanted to be a coolie and that she wanted to take up arms.

On the sixth day, when she had almost given up waiting, Satnam returned and told Jasmeet that he was ready to marry her.

Jasmeet told me that Satnam agreed to marry her because he knew that if he refused, she would go and join the Babbars.[8]

Jasmeet recounted how things panned out after that. 'I started to work with the Khalistan Tiger Force, so there was no reason to choose any other group. Plus they had taken care of me while

I was in jail. In fact, the Babbars had even messaged me while I was in jail, saying that they could get me out by kidnapping DIG Bhullar's son, but I refused their offer.'

After their marriage, Satnam took Jasmeet to the roof of a house in a jungle in Uttarakhand. There was only one bed on the roof. He informed her that he would be sleeping that night while she would be required to stand in one corner of the roof and keep watch.

'I was in a completely different world, away from the luxuries and comforts of my parents' house,' recalls Jasmeet. 'As the night wore on, I could only manage to keep my eyes open for about an hour. Slowly, I started leaning against the boundary wall of the terrace while trying to remain standing, but eventually I fell asleep on a heap of stones close to the wall.'

A few hours later, Jasmeet was woken up by Satnam. The men below had spotted lights and movement in the distance. Nobody wanted to fight; there was not enough ammunition. Therefore, the group packed up and left the safe house immediately. The next day, they heard that the lights and noise had been created by timber smugglers trafficking wood from the forest.

A few weeks after their wedding, Satnam's chest injuries began to worsen. He needed medical attention, but since he refused to go to a doctor himself, Jasmeet made the trips for him and bought him the medical supplies he needed. She also began making regular trips to Punjab around this time to smuggle arms into Uttar Pradesh. It was not a steady life, with the couple changing houses and locations every few months. They shifted from Punjab to Uttar Pradesh and from Uttar Pradesh to Delhi. The Khalistan movement was never far from their motives and minds—in Delhi, for instance, their plan was to secure the release of Harjinder Singh Jinda, but the mission failed after the leader of the mission, Baljeet Singh, was nabbed by the police in Anandpur Sahib.

In January 1992, Jasmeet and Satnam had their first child. The second one was born a year later in 1993.

When the family finally returned to Amritsar from Delhi in the beginning of 1993, the Sikh militancy movement was almost over. Satnam asked Jasmeet to go to his sister's house in Dehradun as he himself would be moving to Pakistan. He had no supporters, no arms and no money left. His plan was to try to get local support in Pakistan and revive the Khalistan movement there. Who was Satnam referring to when he talked about Pakistani support, I asked Jasmeet. She replied readily, 'The Choudhary brothers in Pakistan were smugglers and they were connected to the Inter-Services Intelligence (ISI). Satnam was sure of receiving their help. That's why he wanted to go.'

While they were still in Delhi, Jasmeet had fractured her arm and she couldn't handle taking care of both her kids because of the injury. Satnam called for help from his village, and a young woman came to Delhi to bring back Jasmeet's younger son, a few months old then, to the village until she recovered.

When this young woman returned to Satnam's village with the baby, the news of their presence in the village leaked out. The woman and the infant soon got arrested.

In 1993, Satnam Singh Chinna was caught at the Indo-Pak border and killed in an encounter with the BSF. Jasmeet alleges this to be a fake encounter. That year, Dalbir Singh Randhawa was dismissed from service. 'My father would meet me, as any father would. But he had no involvement with us or with the movement.'

Jasmeet was in Dehradun when she heard of her husband's death. Terrified for the safety of her elder son, she crossed the border and entered Nepal. 'I had wanted to run away to Nepal earlier as well, but whenever I mentioned it to Satnam, he would get angry. He would say, "So many mothers have lost their sons to this movement. Now you want me to run away after their sons are dead?"'

After five months in Nepal, Jasmeet decided to return to India. The man who had sheltered her in Nepal gave her the keys to his home in Gurdaspur. She travelled back and remained in hiding until her neighbours in Gurdaspur informed the police that Satnam Singh Chinna's widow was living there. 'I had no money and no way to earn it. Life was miserable as there was no source of income. I was totally dependent on Khalistani sympathizers who did come forward to help at that time even though the movement was almost in ruins and thousands had been killed.'

Jasmeet was arrested in Gurdaspur in 1995. The policeman who arrested her remembered her father and asked her, 'What have you gained out of all this? Look at yourself! You were a police officer's daughter and so well-read. What have you done to yourself?'

Jasmeet was taken from Ajnala to the B-Division thana at Sultanwind Gate.

Here, she was called to sit on a chair which had some wires spiralling around it. It was an instrument of torture, used to give electric shocks to prisoners. The police first tried to scare her, threatening that they would make her sit on the chair if she didn't speak. 'They kept asking me where Satnam had hidden his arms and money. They wanted to know where I was staying and who might have helped me get here.'

As a consequence of her defiance, she was forced to sit on the notorious chair commonly used for torture in Punjab back in those days. Jasmeet recounts being asked jeeringly if she would move while being seated on the chair. In response, she brazenly retorted to the police officer, 'Why don't you tie my arms, Uncleji?' So, they did tie her arms to the chair.

The first few shocks were painless, so numb was Jasmeet. 'I kept praying and asking for strength in order to keep my mouth shut.' A live wire was placed on her hands. She still refused to speak. Finally, they gave her an electric shock in the neck. 'That almost killed me, it was so painful,' recalled Jasmeet. 'But even then I kept my mouth shut. Finally, the officers told me, "O shedanee (crazy woman), make some noise, otherwise the SP himself will come and torture you."' Jasmeet still resisted and, this time, the live wires were placed right on her face. 'That was it. It felt like they'd taken the skin off my face. I screamed and screamed. After that, I went numb.'

Jasmeet was later taken to the SP's room. After one look at her, the SP asked his subordinates, 'She looks absolutely fine. Did you even touch her?'

'That's when I realized that if I didn't at least pretend to be in pain, they would torture me again and again. So, I screamed and fell on the floor. The SP wanted to know if I had given up any information during the torture. When he was told that I had stayed quiet, he kicked my face and stomach until I couldn't move at all.'

Broken and bleeding, Jasmeet was taken away to her cell. She kept begging the policemen for some water. By this time, the same policemen who had tortured her endlessly were strangely emotional. They seemed to remember the strong figure of her father.

'We were looking for you for years. We even went to UP to look for you,' one of the policemen told Jasmeet. 'Your father was my guru. What have you done to your family? Did you get anything out of it? Thank God you were arrested in Punjab. Had it been in UP, I would have killed you myself and thrown your body into the Gomti.'

Jasmeet was in jail for eight months. By the time she was released, the Khalistan movement had petered out and her world had been literally torn apart. Her husband had been killed and her her younger son was taken away from her by the local authorities and given to Satnam's parents. She grasped the stark reality that there was little left awaiting her return.

Eventually, Jasmeet decided to leave India altogether. She moved to Portugal where she spent the next ten years of her life. But even there, the shadows of 1984 continued to haunt her. The injuries she had sustained while she was in police custody were debilitating, rendering her unable to work. Ten years after she left, Jasmeet was forced to return to India, but it was a country she no longer understood.

Jasmeet now lives in Chandigarh: a closely guarded life, which she leads as privately and as anonymously as she can. She socializes with no one and does not talk to the media at all. When I asked her if she regretted her past decisions to join the Khalistan movement, Jasmeet's answer was decisive, 'I never liked the patriarchal, domesticated life where women are expected to dress up and wait for their husbands and work to just please them. I never wanted jewellery or big houses; I always wanted a challenging life and I lived one.'

In Jasmeet's eyes, the Khalistan movement was justified. 'Most of the things you hear today are rumours. Things got murkier when the sarkari CATS[9] infiltrated the movement. We were young, but no one misbehaved and we were equals in the movement.' After Operation Blue Star, Jasmeet provided assistance to multiple militant outfits, facilitating tasks like relaying information, transporting medical supplies. But she was not a part of any group.[10] It wasn't until she married Satnam and joined his group that she became fully immersed in militant activities.

In our subsequent interactions after my initial conversation with Jasmeet, I visited her one BHK rented home in Chandigarh on a few occasions. During one of these visits, as we sat sipping coffee, she on the sofa that her son had newly bought, Jasmeet said, 'I don't regret my actions. The government was responsible for alienating young people. We did what was required.'

11
Letters from Jail

Kulbir Kaur was hiding.

Along with four other people, she had taken refuge in one of the rooms at Guru Nanak Niwas, the rest house within the Golden Temple complex, during Operation Blue Star. She remained hidden there from 1 June to 6 June 1984.

After the firing incident of 1 June, Kulbir had stepped out of the room in which she had been hiding and had quietly made her way to the main area of the temple. 'I saw a baby feeder covered in blood. It worsened the distress I had been experiencing since the 1978 Nirankari-Sikh Clash.'

On 13 April 1978, a convention was organized in Amritsar that angered activists of the Akhand Kirtani Jatha[1] and the Damdami Taksal.[2] This led to a violent clash between the two sects that left seventeen people, most of them Sikhs, dead.

Traditionally, the Sikhs do not consider the Nirankari sect to be a part of the main Sikh community because they have worshipped other living gurus for over a century. In spite of this, the relationship between the two had been largely peaceful. But the Nirankari massacre of 13 April changed things.

Following the clash, the Akal Takht issued a hukamnama asking all Sikhs to sever ties with Nirankari Sikhs. Additionally, the then chief minister of Punjab, Prakash Singh Badal, ordered the closure of all Nirankari Bhawans in Punjab, although he revoked this order a week later.

The incident is considered to be a turning point in Punjab's modern political history, followed as it was by events like Operation Blue Star which alienated many young Sikhs like Kulbir Kaur. However, on the other hand, such tragic incidents also acted as an impetus for many Sikhs to drift closer to their faith and identity.

Kulbir's family, for instance, had arranged a match for her in the United States of America but she turned it down because the prospective bridegroom asked her to not wear her turban after their wedding.

'For me, the turban is a part of my identity. Initially, Sant Jarnail Singh Bhindranwale used to visit our village every year for a two-day congregation. Like many others, I used to go there for seva, service, with my family, and we would offer donations there. However, this led to the police following me to my college in Hoshiarpur, where they questioned the principal about my activities and demanded that I be handed over to their custody. My principal refused to do so and informed my family about what was happening.'

The matter was eventually resolved, but in retrospect, the incident mirrored how differently militancy in Punjab affected people, depending on their class. In Kulbir's case, she came from an upper-middle class family of Jat Sikhs, with influence and clout. Many, however, were not as fortunate as she was, and it was mostly women who bore the brunt of political power during the Khalistan movement and the fallout of 1984. The CATS, for instance, would often arrive at the doorsteps of many in Punjab, asking insolently for food while pointing loaded guns at the women who opened the doors of the house. In other cases, women were carefully handpicked by the CATS for rape and sexual abuse.

Family members were frequently arrested instead of those actually wanted by the police and then held as hostages until the person sought was produced. Short-term detention was also used punitively. Former detainees and the family members of these detainees have described being subjected to frequent short-term arrests as a form of harassment. But women were always the easiest targets—being picked up for sexual torture, sometimes simply to spite the husbands, fathers, brothers and sons who had wronged the state in the eyes of the law. Often, these incidents occurred even when the men in question were innocent.

On 19 May 1990, Balbir Kaur (name changed),[3] a young college student in Ludhiana, was on her way to the bus stop when two men in plain clothes began following her on a scooter. As she reached the bus stop, these two men stopped her, saying, 'We know you. No point in running away as we are police officials.'[4]

When she refused to believe them, they showed their identity cards to her. One of them was Harvinder Singh, from the Saddar Police Station, and the other was Bhola Sen, an employee of the Punjab Housing Board. They said to her, 'We know you are Gurmeet's sister from Ghawadi village.' Balbir was terrified. Her younger brother, Gurmeet, had been mixed up with the law for years, mostly on fabricated charges. In 1986, he had been tortured for days, hung from a ceiling and his genitals burnt with a candle.

Balbir was told that she would have to come with the police to the police station and when she refused, they said, 'If you don't, we'll pick you up and take you there.' Feeling helpless, Balbir got on the scooter. She was then taken to the Housing Board Colony in Jamalpur, to House No. 169, which belonged to Amarjit Singh, a real estate dealer.

The policemen demanded that she tell them where her brother was or they would rape her. 'I told them I had no idea where he was. When they heard that, they asked me to take off my clothes. I refused. Then they tore my clothes off. Harvinder Singh raped me.' The policemen then left Balbir alone in the darkened room, locking the door behind them. They returned what seemed like hours later, with food and liquor, and a third man in uniform. The three men ate and drank loudly in the next room, before returning to rape Balbir again and again. Gurmeet, Balbir's brother, was murdered in an encounter with the police later that same year.

Balbir's horrific trauma is but one microcosmic incident revealing how Sikh women were treated by the law in the aftermath of 1984. Across Punjab, there are horrendous stories of how women were raped by the police and some even forcibly married off to militants. Women lost their agency to decide. Although there were some women who showed a predisposition towards militancy, it was only police brutality that prompted them to join the armed struggle.

THE KAURS OF 1984

In one of my conversations with Kulbir Kaur, I asked her why she had picked up guns, to which she replied, 'Picking up guns was more liberating, especially in the face of regular harassment at the hands of the army and then the police. And we had seen Harmandir Sahib after the attack; I can never forget that scene, everything around our holiest shrine in rubble.'

Kulbir's story is a long and harrowing one. 'By the evening of 2 June 1984, there was chaos at the Golden Temple. Curfew orders were in place, but the security forces were still not preventing pilgrims from entering the complex. It seemed as if they wanted to inflict maximum damage and casualty; otherwise, why would they allow pilgrims inside the complex when they had unquestionable intelligence about the attack?'

After 3 June 1984, Kulbir did not leave the room inside which she had been hiding. 'The scenes inside the Golden Temple were perplexing, horrifying and difficult to describe. In the scorching heat of June, there was no electricity, no water and no food for anyone. All the main supplies were cut. Most of the people in the rest houses were regular visitors who had nothing to do with the movement, and with curfew orders in place, they were forced to stay where they were. Women who had been visiting the temple with their children were trapped. There were hungry babies who wouldn't stop crying. Gunfire and bombs kept many children awake and terrified. It felt as though we were in a warzone.

'On 5 June, the army finally made announcements telling the people to leave, but I sensed foul play. Four people who had been hiding with me in my room wanted to leave and go to the Golden Temple. Despite my efforts to intervene, Gurmeet Singh, an acquaintance, remained resolute in his decision, unaffected by any attempts to dissuade him. He wanted to see the Golden Temple, but just when he stepped downstairs, he was killed by a bust shot.'

In the early hours of 6 June, someone known to Kulbir, whom she wished to keep anonymous, told the remaining people in the room that it was suicidal to stay in the room and urged everyone to leave, emphasizing the need to survive and fight back against the system once the operation concluded. Their call to action was clear: to not only strengthen the movement from outside by preparing to seek revenge for desecration of their holiest shrine but also fight inside the movement. 'I did not want to leave the temple complex and instead wanted to stay back and fight against the army, make them pay for the damage they had done to the holiest of our shrines. I tried to convince the men in the room to stay and fight. A middle-aged man present in the room told me to channelize my anger and seek revenge for what had happened. And then I came down along with the others, picked up the guns of the dead militants and escaped from the complex.'

Kulbir escaped from Guru Nanak Niwas and made her way to the SGPC quarters. From there, using a back door, she left the Golden Temple complex through the Baghwali Gali. With her were four others and the group hid in one of the houses in the lane for two hours. There were already quite a lot of people there when Kulbir and the others arrived—about sixty or seventy distraught Sikhs cramped in a tiny room. After that, Kulbir escaped to another house in Sultanwind area, which was nearly a mile and half away. There, she stayed with her sister and an acquaintance for the next few days. 'We were staying under a tin shed; it was unbearably hot and sometimes we did not even have water to drink. My pregnant sister left Amritsar seventeen days after Operation Blue Star. She went to our parents' home in Hoshiarpur. My brother-in-law, meanwhile, had been staying with a noted doctor in Amritsar, but he was picked up by the CRPF and taken for questioning after the doctor's neighbours complained about him.'

But Kulbir's brother-in-law, Kanwar Singh Dhami, was a well known figure in the inner circles of Sikh militant groups. He would run an organization called the Akal Federation. It was one of the quiet organizations, using the power of words and propaganda in the Khalistani movement. One day after the CRPF picked him up, he was brought to the Army camp. While in custody, he approached an Indian Army captain and said that he was Longowal's associate and that he had been detained wrongly. The captain allowed him to send a chit to his friends that said 'Bring back your men.' An hour later, Kulbir and Dhami's friends came and staged a dharna for his release after which he was let off.[5]

Kulbir's parents had somehow managed to send a message to Amritsar to inform her that she should not return home; men from the Indian Army were regularly visiting their home and it wouldn't be safe for her. 'They told me that the army had already picked up my elder sister and there was no way they could protect me if I went back. So, it would be better if I didn't go back home.'

For over thirty days, Kulbir had nowhere to go. She and her brother-in-law hid in different villages across Punjab before they finally decided to cross the international border and enter Pakistan via Bhagtana Tullianwala, in Gurdaspur. Their contact in Pakistan was duly informed about their arrival.

Pakistan was only a stone's throw away, if one knew how to swim across the mighty Ravi River, which was in spate due to the monsoon. Five others would be making the crossing along with Kulbir and her brother-in-law; out of them all, only one person knew how to swim.

This person—who remains anonymous—swam across the river to get help for the rest of the party from Pakistani rangers. But no rangers were found anywhere. Instead, there were some locals herding buffalo near the river. They were the next best option. Kulbir recalls holding the tails of buffaloes for support as they waded across the river. 'When we reached the other side of the border, the village chief informed the villagers that there were some guests from India who had arrived. Many of them came to stare at us like we were strange specimens.' When Kulbir changed into a salwar kameez from the men's kurta-pyjama that was her usual attire, everyone was shocked. Until now, no woman had dared to make the risky border crossing, and that too in the company of men.

Shortly after they crossed the Ravi, Dhami and the other men were taken by security personnel for questioning. In all probability, it was the ISI that conducted these interrogation sessions, but Kulbir says she doesn't know who those officers were.

'I had no clue who these officers were and I had no contacts there in Pakistan. The atmosphere in Punjab had been such that I crossed over to Pakistan for safety and we thought many others would follow us. But no one came. My family had told me that they couldn't protect me. The only choice I had was to cross the border. I was under the impression that after we reach Pakistan, many others from Punjab would follow and we would go back with arms and ammunition to fight in India, but they gave nothing,' said Kulbir.

The entire group, including Kulbir, was later detained at a guest house near Lahore.

'The intelligence officer in Pakistan knew the exact details of where we had been hiding inside the Guru Nanak Niwas and about the role of my brother-in-law in all this.' This realization shook Kulbir because it meant that ISI recruits had been present inside the Golden Temple complex during Operation Blue Star. 'One of the ISI agents told my brother-in-law that jails in Pakistan are not safe for women, so it would not be appropriate for me to be in jail alone. He demanded that I should either be sent back to India or be married off to my brother-in-law; that was the only way we could stay together. Because I had no other choice, I agreed to get married to my brother-in-law in Pakistan.'

While in Pakistan, Kulbir shuttled between Sialkot and Lahore. 'The ISI did more harm to the Khalistani movement than any good because they didn't provide the militants with arms. They wanted everything to be done in accordance to their liking. We were mere pawns. They wanted targets and action, but as per their discretion. They never supported us financially.'

Kulbir entered Pakistan a total of three times, and the last time she entered, she brought Paramjit Singh Panjwar, leader of the separatist group Khalistan Commando Force, with her in 1989. Forty-one-year-old Paramjit was wanted in India for reviving the Sikh insurgency.[6] Kulbir finally came back to India in late 1989.

I met Kulbir for the first time at the orphanage that she runs in Chandigarh. She was sitting in front of a heater and drying her hair. I was working for Amnesty International's Halt the Hate

Project[7] at that time. Kulbir grilled me for a while about where I came from, my work and family and why I wanted to talk to her about an incident that was three decades old. Once she understood that I was a researcher, Kulbir held nothing back. She opened up to me quickly and shared the letters she had written from jail to different people. 'These letters will tell you about my journey.'

When I went through the letters myself, I saw that they highlighted, at great length, the torture that Kulbir suffered at the hands of Punjab Police.

Upon her return from Pakistan, Kulbir went underground from 1989 to 1993, spending time in Haryana, Guwahati and Gujarat, before finally moving to Himachal Pradesh where she found employment at the Akal Academy Baru Sahib.

In the early hours of 19 May 1993, however, Kulbir was arrested by the Punjab Police along with her five-year-old son, who was studying in the same school where she was working. 'I argued with the police about why they had arrested my son, and they told me that their sahib had given the orders, which meant that higher-ranking police officials were involved. On the way from Himachal to Tarn Taran, Inspector Ramnath ill-treated me and called me names. When I protested and asked him to behave, he pulled out his gun and held it against my forehead. My son was terrified and started crying.'

Later that evening, Kulbir was produced in front of Senior Superintendent of Police (SSP) Ajit Singh Sandhu. With him were other officials of Tarn Taran district.

'When I was brought into the room, I saw my husband sitting on the floor in shackles. He was bleeding. DSP Bhikiwind introduced me to the others present in the room and told them that I was upset with Inspector Ramnath's behaviour. To this, the SSP replied, "*Eh dali sanu kanoon sikhayegi*? Now this pimp is going to teach us the law?"'

The SSP constituted an interrogation team which included him and DSP Bhikiwind. He then ordered that Kulbir's husband shouldn't be allowed to sleep for seven straight days. Each team was to interrogate and torture him for three hours and then hand over the charge to the next team. Kulbir was to be brought in every now and then and humiliated and tortured in front of her husband in order to break him. 'The senior cop instructed the teams to go hard on me and my husband. He instructed them to torture us in a way that we would beg them for death.'

Kulbir and her husband were taken to the adjoining room, where she was asked to sit. Then, her husband's clothes were removed. They used a ghotna, a four-foot-long pestle that is normally used for grinding spices, as their instrument of torture. The ghotna was placed between Kulbir's husband's thighs and then his ankles were tied forcibly together.[8]

'My husband was screaming. It was excruciating. Then SSP Sandhu started calling me names and slapping me. Every three hours, a new team would come in and repeat the drill. Some of them also gave us electric shocks. They used ropes to torture my husband. Within hours, he was bleeding profusely. His skin was peeling off. At the end of every shift, they would ask us how we were feeling.'

Kulbir says that the officials at the Crime Investigation Agency (CIA) Tarn Taran took special permission from their seniors to torture Kulbir in front of her husband in order to break him. 'I was asked to sit on an electric chair and my hands were tied with my dupatta. A lady constable electrocuted me in my eyes, ears and tongue. My body went numb and I passed out. They revived me by slapping my face.' So horrifying was the degree of torture that the women constables eventually refused to carry on with it.

After this, DSP Bhikiwind ordered Assistant Sub-Inspector (ASI) Rajwinder Kaur to take charge of the interrogation and torture. ASI Kaur first reprimanded her juniors and said, 'I have finished many like Kulbir Kaur. I know how to deal with people like her. And that is why I get promotions.'

The torture went on for days. The police wanted information on terrorists, which the couple refused to give. Kulbir said, 'A consignment of arms had come to Gujarat and because my husband was arrested from Gujarat, they thought he had something to do with it. They wanted us to give them information about the consignment. The more we refused, the harder we were beaten.'

In a letter that Kulbir wrote years later, she recalls that at that time, she was pregnant. The beatings she sustained while in police custody forced her to miscarry.

'How can we forget what you did to us in the jail and in the police stations?' Kulbir would write later. 'My husband was in shackles for a week and he was not allowed to sleep. We were treated in the most undignified and inhumane way. They threw salt on our wounds. My child and I were forced to see my husband getting tortured. I was tortured in front of him so that he could be mentally tortured. My five-year-old was made to witness all of this.

'We were not given any warm clothing during the harsh winter, not even our child. The CIA building was in a jungle, so it was not just the cold, but there were many snakes and rats that infested the complex. At night, rats would often jump on us and sometimes even bite us while we were sleeping.'

On 15 August 1993, the police asked the couple to surrender. However, this had to be postponed because by this time the bodies of both husband and wife bore visible signs of torture. In addition, both Kulbir and her husband refused to surrender. SSP Sandhu visited them and tried to convince them to surrender. 'Why don't you agree to surrender?' he asked. When the couple refused, the SSP replied, 'I am a Jat (a dominant community in Punjab) and I will make sure you do surrender.'

'My husband then asked him, "Why don't you kill us?" And SSP Sandhu replied, "Once you surrender, we will send you home without any case against you, but then we will get you killed by the CATS and say that you were killed by the ISI. We will get you killed and we will be rewarded for it, and the message will go out that Punjab Police neutralized a hardcore separatist. Or we will force you to speak against the movement and you will be killed after that. Then we will use a letter pad belonging to one of the militant groups and put blame on them."'

On 26 January 1994, the police planned a press conference in which they hoped that the couple would surrender. But Kulbir and her husband again refused to do so, enraging the authorities. 'SSP Umrananagl tried to convince me and my husband to surrender and go back home. He said, "If you quit all of this and don't blame anyone for the torture, we won't kill you. But if you don't, then we will throw you in the river. The movement is over now; there is no one left. I was also a part of it but now I have a better life. If you listen to us, your life will be smooth and we will arrange a house and money for you." My husband then asked the SSP, "You might have made millions of rupees in rewards, but at the end of the day, you also eat the same roti.'"

In one of her letters, Kulbir wrote that the CIA Tarn Taran was full of sad stories. She remembers a baba, an old man who often used to shout for help from the window of his tiny cell. He even begged Kulbir for help, saying, 'These monsters have looted gurdwaras. God will punish them. One day, they will go mad. They will beg for death but God will not grant their wish.' After he died, Kulbir got to know that the man was Baba Charan Singh (Beed Sahib Wale), known for his dedicated service to gurdwaras.

'There were many rumours in the CIA Tarn Taran after Baba's death. Once I heard that the police was using Baba's car to go to Pathankot, but they had an accident and were badly injured. Two of them suffered spinal injuries and were never able to walk again,' said Kulbir.

In her letters, Kulbir also mentioned a young girl whom she met while at CIA Tarn Taran's custody and whom she missed dearly. The girl's name was Gurpreet Kaur and she belonged to Shafipur, a village near Tarn Taran. Gurpreet was incredibly beautiful, and even though she was still not eighteen, she had been married to a militant by the name of Balwinder Singh. Along her with relatives, Gurpreet was detained in various police stations across Punjab for nearly eight months. Eventually, Kulbir wrote, Gurpreet couldn't take it any more and tried to escape from the Bhikiwind Police Station. Unfortunately, she was caught and brought back. Helpless and hopeless, she drank phenyl that same night. The police left her in Kulbir's arms.

'The police told me, "She is one of you. Take care of her or she will die soon." I gave her lime water and messaged her feet for the entire night. She kept vomiting incessantly. But two days later, she started recovering. I made sure Gurpreet drank enough water. While Gurpreet was in my cell, my husband was in a kal kothri, a solitary confinement cell in Bhikiwind. He was told by the police that his wife and son were both dead.'

After two days, Gurpreet was taken to Bhikiwind, where she was shackled and kept in a cell designated for male inmates. Kulbir's husband caught sight of Gurpreet there, wearing Kulbir's chappals, and only when he saw those chappals did he realize that Kulbir was still very much alive and at CIA Tarn Taran.

Kulbir's husband last saw Gurpreet with a DSP and Inspector CIA Bhikiwind, Ravi Bhushan, in front of his cell. 'One of the officers said that they were taking her to *Har ki Nehar*, river Harike. We don't know what happened to her, but a few days later, we heard she was dead,' Kulbir remembered.

Kulbir told me that many of her friends who had been in jail with her had been killed in fake encounters. One such woman was Surjeet Kaur, principal of Model School Tarn Taran and mother of a one-year-old.[9] Arrested on charges of sheltering militants, Surjeet was tortured until the end of her days.

Kulbir recalls being with Surjeet for about ten days in jail, and every day, she would be tortured almost three to four times. She often heard Surjeet shouting that no male police personnel should touch her, but no one paid her any heed. She was beaten up by male officers with sticks. They also used the ghotna on her. They would drag her by pulling her breasts. Her interrogation was done by SP (Operations) Khubi Ram, DSP D. Gurmeet Singh, Inspector Ramnath and ASI Tarlochan Singh Walia.

Kulbir Kaur witnessed Surjeet's last moments when she was beaten badly and dragged out of her cell at around 8 p.m. She was crying like a child for her son and shouting his name, 'Monu! Monu!'

'She screamed her final wish to me, "Kulbir, you have to take care of my child now!"' recalls Kulbir. 'Surjeet was innocent. She had nothing to do with the violence.'

It's worth noting that in Punjab, it was common for innocent families to provide shelter or be forced to do so unknowingly to militants. Sadly, these families often faced police wrath. Three men, allegedly embroiled in militant activities, were staying at Surjeet's house, even though she and her husband were entirely uninvolved.

Tragically, on the same night following Surjeet's demise, around 3 a.m., her husband and all three men were forcefully taken and later reported as casualties of a supposed terrorist encounter.

In her letters, Kulbir writes that she met different militant families in prison, including that of the greatest and most dreaded Sikh militant, Gurbachan Singh Manochahal.[10]

'I along with my husband and son were kept in the same cell, and this cell was opposite the interrogation room. Every day, we would see four to five people being brought to that room for interrogation. Some were released after they negotiated how much to pay the police for their release, and those who couldn't or didn't want to pay were either killed or framed in false cases.'

By the end of April 1994, CIA Ropar was buzzing with arrested Sikh militants, separatist leaders and police informers. The police had begun building pressure on their informants to get more and more militants arrested. However, by now the movement had died down and there were barely any leads for the informants to provide to the police. Where the informants failed to perform, they became targets of the police's wrath themselves. The police needed at least some militants to hound and pursue because that activity not only gave them power, but it also gave them uncontrolled finances and promotional gains. As the pressure on them mounted, some of these informants became turncoats, and in some cases, either out of anger or to finish off any evidence, the police killed them too.

In her eleven months in illegal detention, Kulbir Kaur wrote more than sixty letters, all of them addressed to holders of political power at the time, including Simranjit Singh Mann, the SGPC, Congress leader Jagmeet Singh Bara, activist Bimla Dang, Comrade Satpal Dang and the jail superintendent and the DC of Patiala. She highlighted in graphic details the inhumane torture carried out by the Punjab Police. Kulbir wrote to the then head of Punjab Police, K.P.S. Gill, as well. In her letters to Gill, she sent details of the incidents of torture that she had witnessed in jail and appealed for a court-based inquiry. She wrote, 'I am not scared of death; if you have a gun then I have my pen with me. We are fighting for truth and justice, unlike you who are fighting for lies and personal gains. I believe in the courts of law and I will demand justice from them.' She recalls the mango tree in front of her cell in one of her letters. 'If that tree could talk, it would tell you horrible stories of how many people were hanged and killed there. From 2 September to 9 April, I had seen men from different communities being hung from that tree.'

On 29 March 1994, Punjab Police staged the surrender of Kanwar Dhami. Dhami was produced before K.P.S. Gill at a press conference and instructed to touch Gill's feet after officially surrendering. However, despite the presence of the media, Dhami refused to read the statement given to him by the police. Instead, he declared, 'As a staunch supporter of Khalistan, I prefer death to surrender.'

Dhami was swiftly apprehended by the police, but not before he defiantly shouted a pro-Khalistan slogan. Later that evening, the police asked him to retract his statement, which he adamantly refused. He even compared K.P.S. Gill to Aurangzeb. Consequently, Dhami was charged with waging war against the state.

In July 1997, Kulbir Kaur Dhami was released from jail, acquitted of all charges.

She started visiting the homes of Sikh families who had been a part of the militant movement. 'I wanted to meet these people and understand how they were living and if there was any additional support that they needed. After Surjeet's death, it had been playing on my mind that there must be many children like Monu and many single mothers too. I simply wanted to help them. There were many women in Punjab who were harassed and they were constantly shifting places, looking for safety. People were scared to keep them in their homes.'

By the end of 1997, twenty-five people joined Kulbir and together they started a trust to help the destitute children and widows of erstwhile militants.

'My children are not sympathetic towards me or the movement. My elder son moved abroad and married a foreigner. My younger son is shifting jobs. My daughter was born in Jalandhar, and sixteen hours after my delivery, the police got to know about us.

We had to leave Jalandhar. The authorities in Baru Sahib said I couldn't keep my daughter with me as she was very young. At that time, she was staying with a family I knew. I had told them that I would take her back with me after six months, but I got arrested meanwhile.'

In spite of her story though, Kulbir says, 'I have no regrets about my past, it was the need of that time. My parents' family suffered huge financial losses and faced regular torture. Those were dark days.'

12
Widows in Delhi

In Delhi, circumstances took a difficult turn for the widows of the anti-Sikh massacre. Some were dealing with new patriarchs while others were struggling to survive against the odds. For months after the massacres, most of these women had no roof over their heads. No medical attention was given towards their health nor was any counselling done for their post-traumatic stress. Women like Darshan Kaur, who had dared to speak the truth to the power that was the Congress leadership, were regularly called in by senior officials to record their statements. Darshan's statement was also recorded multiple times and she was even asked to change it. 'The officials used to ask me intimidating questions and tried to put words in my mouth. They wanted me to change my testimony.'

THE KAURS OF 1984

Most of these women were not educated; many had never stepped out of their homes. They responded to the continuum of patriarchy as they had been conditioned to do so—providing thumb impressions to false statements, and in the case of rape survivors, staying silent because they were commanded to do so. They were, in many ways, the first casualties of the anti-Sikh massacres, yet they remain invisible even today.

Unsurprisingly, male voices have long since dominated the early narratives that gained public attention after 1984. It is only now that those of others, including women and children, have begun adding their stories to what happened in 1984. With the rise of women's voices, in particular, have come a slew of new, intimate and previously unknown histories through which alternate realities have begun to emerge.

Three days after Darshan shifted to the Farash Bazar Camp in Shahdara, she was reunited with her youngest son who had been missing since the day her husband had been attacked. Darshan learned that a woman in her neighbourhood had protected her son from the mob on 1 November by hiding him in her house. Her neighbour had searched for Darshan in different camps across the city before finally locating her at the Farash Bazar Camp, where she was sharing a room in the police quarters with two other families. A week later, Darshan's husband's elder brother's wife also returned from Alwar and joined them at the camp; her husband's sisters were also living with them in the same room.

When Darshan's father finally found her at the camp, he asked his daughter to return with him. But Darshan refused. 'My husband is gone. His family is my responsibility now,' she said.

'My father tried to explain to me that widows of young sons are not very welcome in the families of their late husbands. "They will not be the same with you as they were," he said.' Darshan, however, stuck to her decision.

Remembering her time in the camp, Darshan says that it was full of victims and survivors and that there were no arrangements that had been made for any of them. 'The bathrooms were overflowing all the time; there was no water. It seemed as though after murdering our families, the government had just abandoned us. The camps were mostly managed either by NGOs or by the Delhi Sikh Gurdwara Management Committee; there was almost zero government support. It was a tormenting experience at the camp. Most of us only talked about the number of men who had died in our respective families. Every day, in that open ground and in the corridors of the under-construction quarters, we would hear the screams of mothers, wives and daughters crying all the time. We were living in constant fear and we were living with the daily pain of having lost our families.

'I spent weeks sitting alone and thinking about my husband and the time we had spent together. People in the camp had started talking about my mental health. Most of them thought I had gone mad because I was mostly sitting alone and talking to the trees. I have very good memories of my husband. Sometimes, I used to forget that he is no more. Most of my days went by thinking about how we spent our last Diwali.'

Soon after, Darshan's father-in-law, a man of otherwise few words, claimed himself as the custodian of all that belonged to his sons. When the authorities started making a list of victims for the sake of paying compensations to their kith and kin, Darhsan's father-in-law did not include her name as the beneficiary of her deceased husband. Instead, he told the officers that his younger son was unmarried.

'At first, I decided to stay silent. A few days later, however, I saw my kids being discriminated against, and then I could stay silent no longer. I confronted my father-in-law despite his questions about why I wanted the money at all. He told me that he was the man of the house now and that he would provide for everyone. Those who had gone were his sons first, so he had the first right on the compensation,' Darshan recounted. 'When my parents visited the camp, I told them everything. My father again offered to take me home. He said he would speak to the officials and get my name enrolled in the list of people who would be compensated. But I continued to stay in the camp. I was a widow, an outcast to most.'

Darshan Kaur stayed in the camp for six months, surviving on the little help that came from the Delhi Gurdwara Management Committee and from other civil society organizations. A local activist helped her to move out of the camp and into one of the hurriedly built quarters in Tilak Vihar. It was termed a colony, but in reality, it was nothing more than a ghetto. The Sikh women who moved to Tilak Vihar were women who had been left with nothing. They had no homes to return to. But the quarters in Tilak Vihar were not homes either. They had no electricity, no electrical fittings, no windows and no water. All the women were asked to pay a security deposit of a thousand rupees. For most, it would take weeks to arrange that kind of money. Yet again, Darshan's life changed, as did the lives of hundreds of women like her. Where they had never stepped out of their homes before, they now became working mothers and breadwinners, replacing their lost husbands and fathers.

'It was very challenging initially,' said Darshan. 'We were harassed by men almost everywhere. From police officers to government officers, and in fact those who worked in banks as well—all of them tried to be our guardians. It's difficult for women to work in a normal situation and ours was a different case. We were widows of traitors, that's what they called us. After my husband's death, I have killed myself every day. Society made me feel as if I am nonexistent and unwanted.'

In March 1987, Darshan received her appointment order along with twenty-five other women who had done a sit-in protest outside the residence of the then Lieutenant Governor of New Delhi demanding employment. Some of these women were given employment at the Karkardooma Court and others were sent to work in different hospitals across Delhi. Darshan was hired by Guru Teg Bahadur Hospital, in the Trans-Yamuna area.

Once she started working at the hospital, Darshan's life got a little better as money began coming directly to her. She could buy things for her family and start to rebuild her life. The rigours of her daily life, however, became a little harder. Back in those days, public transport was not the same as it is today. Darshan had to leave home very early in the morning, at around 6 a.m., to be on time for her duty at the hospital. She also had to change two buses every day and it was almost a two-hour-long journey. She would often get very late in returning home as well. Darshan recalled that on one particular winter night, when she was late in returning from work, the bus dropped her and one of her colleagues at Tilak Nagar. As Darshan and her friend walked through the neighbourhood, they sensed the presence of two men shadowing their every move. When one of the men dared to extend his hand towards Darshan, she erupted into a flurry of shouts, bravely defending herself. The men then tried to run away, but Darshan caught hold of one of them. She removed her chappal and beat him black and blue. The man was later handed over to the police.

The next day, while at work, she narrated the entire incident to a doctor who would travel from Subhash Nagar in New Delhi, which is close to Darshan's house. Appalled, the doctor told Darshan to tell all the other women who came from Tilak Nagar that they could travel with him every day.

He was a young, unmarried doctor and was very helpful to the women from Tilak Vihar. He helped Darshan a lot on numerous occasions. In fact, he even changed his duty schedule a lot of times so that he could pick and drop the women from Tilak Vihar. He once asked Darshan about her family and kids. He told her that if she needed any help, she could let him know. He said he wanted to help her with the education of her kids.

As per Darshan, there was a silent bond that grew between her and the doctor. She used to respect him immensely for everything that he did for her, but then the doctor fell for her. They continued to exchange smiles, but Darshan did not speak much to him for months. 'When I sensed some change in his behaviour, I stopped talking to him and started using public transport again,' said Darshan.

Then one day, the doctor confronted her and asked her why she was avoiding him. When Darshan did not respond, he expressed his love for her and proposed to her. But Darshan refused him point-blank and said, 'I can't cheat on my husband and I can't live without my kids.'

Soon after this incident, Darshan got her duty changed and for the next few months, she studiously avoided the doctor.

'Maybe he was in love with me and would have taken care of me, but I had my doubts,' said Darshan as she recalled the entire incident. 'I was a mother of three and I worried about what would happen if he didn't accept my kids later. What if the relationship ended badly for me? And what would my children think of me once they were older? And that doctor was young and successful too; he would've gotten many girls in his life. But now, sometimes I think, what if I was wrong? But all of that is history now.

'There are so many ifs and buts for women in our society that at times, even the women themselves don't want to do things which can make their lives better or which can make them happy. We often make ourselves sad in order to make others happy, but in the end, no one is actually happy. All they have are complaints. The reality is that men want to control us. I think that makes them happy,' Darshan added.

Six years after the massacre, Darshan was summoned by the Karkardooma Court to attend the hearing of her case against H.K.L. Bhagat. When Bhagat was summoned to the court for the first time, he complained of chest pain. The presiding judge remarked dryly, 'How convenient it is for politicians to be afflicted by pain.'

Darshan's journey to identify Bhagat in court was long and lonely. Constant attempts were made to force her to change her statements and testimony. At one point, Atma Singh Lubana, appointed by the Delhi Gurdwara Management Committee to accompany the female survivors of 1984 to court, came to her with a bag bulging with cash. He told Darshan, 'Take this money. For how long will you live in this mess? Think about your sons. Keep this money and we will also buy you a house in Rajouri Garden.' But Darshan rejected the offer. A few weeks later, as she was coming out of court, she was nearly shot dead by three unknown men on a motorcycle. Atma Singh Lubana himself, along with twenty other men, attacked her at the gurdwara, sending Darshan to the hospital for ten days. From death threats to actual attempts on her life, Darshan Kaur faced it all, but she never wavered in her mission to fight for the truth. In the midst of a crowded courtroom, she took only minutes to identify Bhagat. Pulling off her chappal, she pointed it at Bhagat and declared, '*Yehi tha bilkul, yehi hai*, judge sahib. This is definitely him, this is him.' Darshan went on to testify that after hiding her husband, she had seen and heard a mob shouting, '*Maro, maro*! Kill, kill!' She asserted that a white ambassador[1] car had come to the Trilokpuri area in the afternoon and that the residents of the locality had said that a local politician had arrived. 'I also went to see who it was and I saw a man in goggles, accompanied by Congress leader Rampal Saroj and some policemen. The neta (leader) urged the mobs to kill the Sikhs. They said that there should be no one left.'

Yet, legal battles were not the only tragic moments in Darshan's life. Abandoned by her in-laws, and too wrapped up in the sorrows of the past to give love a second chance, Darshan Kaur began working to try and give her children, the new focus of her life, a better world.

But the impact of 1984 on her children was much deeper than expected. 'My children were bullied and taunted at school; they were called fatherless and even children without a daddy. Teachers treated them differently as well.' Darshan also thinks that her sudden entry into the workforce had an adverse impact on her children. Without a male guardian in their lives, and with their mother gone from the house for long hours every day, the children turned wayward and, eventually, they dropped out of school. 'A regular exposure to hurt, humiliation and social isolation made them sink into a world of their own. Depressed and alone, they began having trouble eating and sleeping as they grew older,' rued Darshan.

Today, Darshan lives in her small 200-square-feet house at Raghubir Nagar with her three sons, three daughters-in-law and seven grandchildren. Two of her sons work as autorickshaw drivers and one of them is factory worker.

'Not for a single day have I forgotten what happened to my family and to those of all the others. We are living a hellish life with no justice. Our men were killed and our homes were looted. We were robbed of whatever we had. And they want us to forget and move on. Do you think that's possible? I will only get closure when I close my eyes.'

~

'Here are the Sikhs! Kill them! Cut them!' chanted the mob.

Satwant recognized most of the people in the mob. They were the Hindu residents of her area, men she had once addressed as brothers and uncles. She had known them since her childhood, when she had been the same age as her elder son.

'For many years after the massacre, these sounds echoed in my ears, but I had no time to grieve,' said Satwant when she spoke about the events of 1984. After the massacre, her mother fell sick and her father returned to alcohol. Satwant lived in a camp with her family for a few months, completely dependent on the support of NGOs. 'It was at the camp that I first started getting panic attacks. To divert my mind, I began visiting a music teacher who agreed to teach me for free. Soon after I had my second child, I began performing at night jagrans[2] in order to make ends meet. But because of this, I had to leave the camp.' She faced societal pressure to leave due to the stigma attached to her profession as a singer, especially for a widow. It was frowned upon for a widow to dress up and perform.

'I got my first job through my mentor and these programmes have certain dress requirements. I had to wear a red suit, which many in the camp did not like. After all, I was a widow and my dead husband could very well get offended with my wearing a red suit. How dare I do something like that?

'When I sang for the first time in a hotel, there were so many well-dressed people there—men with their wives and children. I had never had such an opportunity. I closed my eyes and sang. I still remember that I sang *"Aaj fir jeene ki tamanna hai"*. When I finished the song, the audience started clapping. My eyes filled with tears. That was the best moment of my life. I still get goosebumps when I think of that day. I felt like a star then. I can spend my entire life for that one moment alone.'

Satwant became a regular performer in Delhi's luxury hotels. She started getting invited to sing at ghazal nights and cocktail parties. Soon, outdoor shows followed. Satwant now took on the stage name Tara, meaning a star.

She was undeniably popular, but popularity came with a price. Sometimes, she was away from her kids for weeks. 'I took whatever work came my way; I had no choice because there were so many mouths to feed.'

But the shows were never easy for her. She was often dropped from these shows because many of the organizers thought she was too fat and too dark-skinned.

'Once during an outdoor show in Lucknow, my mother fell sick and was admitted to a hospital. Two days later, she died. Her death was a major setback, but once again, I did not get the time to grieve my mother. Can you imagine how difficult it would be for anyone to go out and perform when your mother's dead body is lying at home? But a cremation also needs money.'

A year later, Satwant moved to a government-allotted accommodation at Raja Garden, which she feels was the worst decision she took since it led to a lot of daily interference by her father. He would keep a watch on her and take away all her money. But Satwant had no choice as her siblings were still too young and she had promised her dying mother that she would take care of her brothers and marry off her sisters.

To fulfil this promise to her mother, she took on so much work that at one point, while performing in a private party in a farmhouse in Gurgaon, she collapsed on the stage. She was hospitalized and was told by the doctors to not sing for the next two months. While she was unwell and recuperating at home, all her savings were used up to run both her own house and that of her father.

'None of my family members were working at that time. My brothers blamed me for being unemployed. They told me that they were embarrassed because of me and that when they stepped out the men in the locality asked them about my rates. I was told by my brothers to either bring money into the house or to take the kids away and leave.'

Satwant also had to arrange money for her sister's wedding. She tried her best but she was unable to put the money together. When she felt that there was nothing else that she could do, she sold her one-room accommodation and used the money from the sale to get her sibling married and to help her younger brother start a scooter repair shop.

'After my sister's wedding, I did not have a house of my own. So I moved in with my brother, but once he got married, they did not allow me to stay with them because of my work. I was once again forced back to the same place where I had started rebuilding my life from a decade ago. But this time, I neither had money nor any work.

'When my elder son, Sonu, was sick, none of my family members came to the hospital to inquire about him. I was appalled by the behaviour of my brothers and sisters. Sonu was hospitalized for a month, but I had no one to take care of him. And when I requested my sister to help, she would sometimes come in for a few hours. My younger son Rajan would spend hours in the hospital sitting beside his elder brother. He would be all alone. Every single day presented a new challenge for me. The doctors would ask for more tests to be done but I barely had any money to foot the bills. My son was also not showing any sign of improvements. He needed better treatment which was expensive and not available in the local hospital. I was struggling to arrange money.

'It was Sonu's thirtieth night in the hospital. I reached a little later than usual and found Rajan sitting alone on the stairs. When

I asked him why he was sitting there, he did not say anything and kept avoiding any eye contact with me.

'I ran towards Sonu's bed, but I couldn't find him there. I thought that perhaps they had shifted him to a different ward. I asked the nurse on duty and she told me to meet the doctor in his cabin.

'I rushed downstairs to meet the doctor and he told me they hadn't been able to save my son. He added that he would arrange for an ambulance to take Sonu's body home.'

Satwant recalls falling apart on hearing this news. She collapsed on the floor and started beating her chest and crying uncontrollably. There was no one by her side. Her younger son came inside the room and held her hands as he sat with her. She didn't even have enough money for Sonu's cremation, and not one person from her family came forward to help her out. It was, in fact, a few of her neighbours who arranged for Sonu's funeral.

For Satwant, it was a nightmare. She felt as though the shadows of 1984 held her in a vice-like grip. Heartbroken and despairing, Satwant retreated into herself, almost forgetting that she had a second child to look after. She took to aimlessly walking the streets for hours or sitting silently in the gurdwara.

'It felt like I was back in 1984. Homeless and penniless, and this time a burden on my young son. I had no work and I wasn't sure where to start. After Sonu's death, my younger son Rajan grew up much before his age. He used to get scared if I wasn't around. I returned to work after a few weeks, but most days were spent waiting in the office for work that paid little to nothing.

'My absence at home impacted my younger son. I was also dealing with depression and was not as attentive as before. He had no one to guide him. He stopped going to school. Things got so bad that we began living by selling one personal item a day at home. Later, my younger soon took up a job.

'One day, while I was returning from the gurdwara, I saw our landlord locking the main door of my house. I rushed to him and begged him for some more time to pay the rent. I told him that once I get work, I would pay all his dues, but he didn't listen. He only allowed me to take some clothes and important items from the house. I took all the pictures we had as well. I sat outside the locked house and waited for my Rajan[3] to return. When he got back home, he asked me why I was sitting outside. But I had no answers for him. So instead, I asked him if he was hungry. When he asked for the key to the house, I broke down and said, "I am sorry." I was crying inconsolably, and then my son took me in his arms and said, "Don't worry Mummy, everything will be fine."

'When none of our relatives agreed to let us stay with them, we went to Bangla Sahib Gurdwara. The next day, my son travelled all the way from Bangla Sahib Gurdwara to his place of work in West Delhi. Before leaving for work, he made me promise that I won't go anywhere. He was worried that something would happen to me if I left the gurdwara. Eventually, after my son used to leave for work, I began to go out and clean the cars of the people outside the gurdwara. Sometimes, the people would give me some money.'

Satwant's life was never the same after 1984. Success came in patches and life was never completely steady. It was an existence that was dreary and marked with loneliness and depression.

Two years after her son was finally married, she stopped working. But she was once again treated as a liability after this. Every month, she had to sell a piece of whatever little jewellery she had and give the money to her son as her share for staying in the house with him. But six months later, when all her jewellery was sold, their relationship started souring and differences turned into daily fights. Her daughter-in-law was pregnant at this time and Satwant did not want to stress her out or cause any discord in her son's marital life. So she quietly gathered what was left of her belongings and left home. She never returned.

Satwant now works as a masseuse for women. She goes door-to-door and offers her services. She lives with her widowed sister and runs the house for both of them.

'I worked so hard all my life without thinking about myself, but look what I got in the end. I have been failed by everyone, and more than being disappointed, I have been hurt. A woman has no life. I was questioned by my father when I was living in his home, by my husband after marriage and after his death, my life was controlled first by my brother and then my son. Women have no world of their own. Men want to control us at every level, every stage in our lives.'

The carnage of 1984 remains a matter of national shame, and the continuing impunity for the massacre has made a mockery of justice. The plight of these women who have been awaiting justice for over three decades reflects not just the absolute failure of the government machinery in delivering swift and timely justice, but also the sad state of human rights in our country.

Epilogue

'Are we not Indian citizens? We have faced atrocities at the hands of our own people.'

The victims of the 1984 anti-Sikh massacre are perpetually advised to put a blanket over their past and persevere in order to build a better future. But is it feasible to forget the past? How can such a forced forgetting be the right path to reconciliation?

For most people, November is a month of festivities. Homes are cleaned, walls painted and facades lit up. But for some, darkness still overshadows their lives. Take, for instance, the example of Joginder Kaur. For her, November is a month of mourning, sadness and plain horror. It is the month during which she lost everything she had.

Epilogue

'On 1 November 1984, my husband was attacked with swords and sticks; he lay on a charpoy in a vegetative state for three days after that. Our children sat with him, refusing to leave him. On the third day, a mob barged into our home and killed him. We lost everything in 1984. Our future, our right to progress, everything. My younger son was in a depression for a long time. One day, he left the house and never returned,' says Joginder Kaur.

It is fair, then, to say that the agony of 1984 has not simply ended with those who lived through those times. If anything, the trauma has descended through succeeding generations, with the children of survivors suffering the untold consequences of the violence wreaked upon their elders.

'I remember hearing the news of violent clashes around my place, but I wasn't worried about us because we did not kill Indira (Gandhi). In some time, however, I realized my mistake. Even the police did not protect us; they were equally complicit in what became a massacre. I can clearly recount how my son and husband were beaten to death with sticks. I left my home with some money and gold. But later, all of my belongings were stolen, and the perpetrators tore my clothes,' Shamni Kaur, another survivor of 1984, told me.

She continued, 'We spent three nights in Chilla Gaon to stay away from what was happening. It has been thirty-five years with no justice whatsoever. We feel helpless. The mob killed our men and raped our women. Our people were burnt to death and our houses were looted. However, the custodians of our protection did not care. It felt like Partition all over again, when nobody cared for the common people.'

Epilogue

In 2014, on the thirtieth anniversary of the massacre, Prime Minister Narendra Modi said, 'Let us not forget that a nation that disregards its history can never create one ... (the Sikh massacre) was not a wound in the heart of any community. It was a dagger in the centuries-old fabric of India's unity ... Our own people were murdered.'[1] Yet in terms of showing the political will to deliver justice, the National Democratic Alliance (NDA) government, muck like its predecessors, has failed to deliver.

In February 2015, the central government accepted the recommendations of a retired Supreme Court judge and set up a Special Investigation Team (SIT) to reinvestigate closed cases. The SIT had a chance to finally deliver accountability for thousands who suffered in the massacre. It raised hopes among the victims and survivors that they would finally get justice. The SIT was headed by Pramod Asthana, an IPS officer of the 1986 batch, along with Rakesh Kapoor, a retired district and sessions judge, and Kumar Gyanesh, an additional deputy commissioner of Delhi Police, as its members.

This SIT promised to be different. After all, it was the first body that was empowered to reopen closed cases and file a chargesheet. It was given six months to complete the exercise. From the beginning, however, its functioning was marked by a lack of urgency and transparency. The team was asked to submit a report in August 2015, within six months of its appointment, but it received three extensions, the last one being till August 2017.

During the course of my research for this book, I met many families who were victims of the 1984 anti-Sikh pogrom. One survivor told me that an FIR had been registered for her husband's

Epilogue

killing. But when she received a call from the SIT in September 2016, instead of being asked about the details of the case, she was asked if she wanted to pursue her case at all.

For more than a decade, much has been made of the 'apology' made by former Prime Minister Manmohan Singh. A few things need to be recalled at this stage: firstly, the 'apology' was issued twenty-one years after the massacre. Secondly, the assertion of regret was made in the course of a debate on the Nanavati Commission[2] report, and not as part of a pre-declared announcement that the prime minister of the country would apologize for what had happened in 1984.

As per Amnesty International's report, 'Thirty-one Years and Waiting, an Era of Injustice for the 1984 Sikh Massacre', first published in 2016, a government-appointed commission said, 'There is evidence on record to prove that the police had quietly collected and disposed the bodies of those whom the mobs were unable to burn. The police went on claiming that only a few hundred had died when the figures ran into thousands.'

Some senior officers manipulated logbooks to cover their tracks while others did not record the stories of the victims which came in from time to time. All this was done in an obvious bid to escape responsibility and charges of dereliction of duty and accountability.

I filed an RTI on 27 January 2016, asking for the Control Room Records of 1984. The Outer District Control Room responded with the statement that the present Control Room had been functioning since 2007 and that the records for 1983, 1984 and 1985 were with the North-West District Control Room.

Epilogue

The same RTI application was forwarded from the Deputy Secretary (Home) to the Public Information Officer (PIO, Delhi Police Headquarters). The PIO (Police Control Room) responded on 1 March 2016, stating that the Control Room records for the years 1983, 1984 and 1985 had been destroyed. However, since two responses were provided to two separate RTI applications, asking for the same information, there seems to be a slight discrepancy regarding the date of destruction of the documents in these two responses. The response to my RTI application indicates that the documents for 1983 (numbered 2283-84 ACP/PCR) were destroyed on 10 April 1986, the documents for 1984 were destroyed on 15 September 1987 and documents for the 1985 were destroyed on 10 April 1986. The response to Ms Himanshi Matta's[3] RTI application indicates that the document for 1983 (numbered 2583-84 ACP/PCR) was destroyed on 10 April 1986, the documents for 1984 were destroyed on 15 September 1987 and the documents for 1985 were destroyed on 25 October 1988.

But the question here is whether any institution can destroy any government data while an investigation is underway, or if this was done on purpose.

Two judicial commissions of inquiry and at least nine committees have been appointed by the central and state governments since 1984 to look into different aspects of the massacre. Many of them have pointed to the complicity of both the police and members of the Congress Party for the killings. Several affidavits submitted to different committees and commissions accused senior Congress leaders Sajjan Kumar and Jagdish Tytler of complicity in the violence. Sajjan Kumar was sentenced to life

Epilogue

imprisonment by the Delhi High Court on 17 December 2018 for his role in the 1984 anti-Sikh massacre. But on 21 September 2023, the families of the victims of the anti-Sikh massacre once again stood heartbroken outside the Rouse Avenue Court in New Delhi. The court had acquitted the former Congress Party MP in a case connected to the 1984 massacre which had resulted in the gruesome murder of seven Sikhs in the Sultanpuri area. Special Judge Geetanjali Goel said, 'Accused Sajjan Kumar is acquitted due to the benefit of doubt.'[4] Despite the acquittal, Sajjan Kumar will remain in jail in another case related to the 1984 anti-Sikh massacre.

When the Justice Misra Commission was formed in 1985, it raised much hope amongst the survivors. But what did the commission do? The commission provided the Congress Party, its members and the government with exoneration. In 1985, the Ranganath Misra Commission was established to investigate 'allegations surrounding organized violence following the assassination of the late Prime Minister, Indira Gandhi'. However, from the beginning, procedural biases tainted its proceedings. The commission allowed police officials and administrators to provide testimony in camera, while simultaneously preventing lawyers representing victims from attending, let alone cross-examining witnesses.

In an attempt to rationalize the initial wave of violence post the prime minister's assassination, the Misra Commission oddly labelled it as 'natural'. Ranganath Misra contended, 'According to Indian tradition, a lady cannot be killed, and she is said to be Avadhya.' Strikingly, the commission absolved senior Congress members of culpability, shifting the blame onto locals. It went to the extent of arguing that senior Congress leaders could not have orchestrated the massacre because, had they been responsible, the violence would have been more severe.

After his role in the commission, Ranganath Misra ascended to the position of Chief Justice of the Supreme Court. In 1993, following his retirement, he assumed the inaugural leadership of the National Human Rights Commission. Subsequently, five years later, the Congress, now in opposition, nominated him to the Rajya Sabha.[5] In August 2016, the term of the SIT constituted to look into all the closed cases of the anti-Sikh massacre was extended a second time, and in February 2017, a third time. In March 2017, the SIT finally told the Supreme Court that it had closed 199 cases it was looking into, and in August 2017, the government stated that another forty-two had been closed. After over two years of investigation, the SIT had filed charge sheets in only twelve cases.

In 2016, I met the head of the SIT at its Khan Market's office in New Delhi. With me were Darshan Kaur, one of the victims of the 1984 massacre, and the advocacy officer for Amnesty International. Darshan Kaur narrated the details of her case to the SIT head and we submitted a copy of Amnesty International India's report on the Delhi massacre along with the recommendations drafted by civil society.

Something peculiar occurred in the office when a clerk, upon noticing me, remarked to his colleague, '*Woh RTI wala Sardar aaya hai.* That Sardar who sends RTI requests is here.' I hadn't met him before, yet he seemed familiar with my identity. He also made another reference, saying, '*Jo hare kurta main bol raha tha,* The one who spoke while wearing a green kurta,' alluding to the

Epilogue

report launch where I had last spoken about the 1984 anti-Sikh massacre.

I'm uncertain whether they genuinely recognized me due to my frequent writing and submission of RTIs or if it was their way of signalling that they were aware of my movements. Nevertheless, the situation felt intimidating.

In August 2017, the Supreme Court constituted a supervisory body comprising two erstwhile Supreme Court judges, Justice J.M. Panchal and Justice K.S.P. Radhakrishnan, to see if the closure of the cases by the SIT was justified. Once again, fixing accountability for the 1984 killings had to wait.

On 11 January 2018, after the supervisory body submitted its report in the apex court, the court decided to set up its own three-member SIT to probe the 186 cases which had not been reopened by the union government's SIT. The new SIT team was headed by a former high court judge, Justice S.N. Dhingra. However, the SIT did not function for nearly ten months as it kept waiting for its third member to be appointed.

As a judge in the Karkardooma District Court, Justice Dhingra had dealt with many cases related to the 1984 massacre. At least sixteen of these cases had resulted in a conviction, the most famous being that of Kishori Lal, who was called 'Trilokpuri's butcher' by the media for his role in killing many Sikhs in Delhi.

In 2018, I, along with the advocacy officer of Amnesty International India, arranged a meeting with Justice Dhingra at his office in the Law Ministry. This time we submitted the civil society's recommendations on what the way forward for the

Epilogue

families should be and our reports as well. Justice Dhingra told us that if we had any case details, we should feel free to share them with him.

Around November 2018, the central government told the Supreme Court that it was not necessary to find a third member for the SIT probing the 1984 cases. The government told a bench of Justices Madan B. Lokur and Deepak Gupta that it had no objection if the two members of the SIT—Justice S.N. Dhingra and serving IPS officer Abhishek Dular—continued with the work.

In an interview published in *Outlook* on 18 January 2020, Justice Dhingra said:

> In January 2019, the Court gave us three months to file our report. Our report had been finalized and submitted to the Union Law Ministry by April-end. I do not know why the government did not submit the report to the Court immediately. I do not know the motivations behind the Centre informing the Court that the report was received in October.

However, he did not reopen any case for reinvestigation because of the omnibus FIRs and also because records are weeded out from the trial court. His report once again highlighted the complicity of the police in the violence against the Sikhs. The report said that the police, the government and the prosecution lacked in submitting their findings before the court at the right time. The Dhingra Committee also highlighted that the then SHO of

EPILOGUE

Kalyanpuri Police Station was complicit in attacking Sikhs and supporting the rioters.

On 15 January 2020, the central government told the Supreme Court that it had accepted the recommendations made by Justice Dhingra. In May 2023, the Central Bureau of Investigation filed a charge sheet in which it said, 'Jagdish Tytler incited, instigated and provoked the mob at the Pul Bangash area on November 1, 1984 which resulted in the killing of three Sikhs.'[6]

Today, there is a kind of restiveness among the Sikh community, both within the country and amongst the Sikh diaspora, over the inexplicable delay in delivering justice to the victims of the 1984 massacres. The first and second generations of victims have grown up to be bitter and angry citizens, and an embittered population is not good either for long-term peace or for the stability of the country. It would be prudent for any government to catch early warning signals when it comes to its people. Those among the culprits who are still alive, must, therefore be punished, failing which, a bad precedent would be set.

The impunity for the 1984 massacre has, however, been used to downplay other incidents of mass violence, notably the 2002 Gujarat massacre and the 2013 massacre in Muzaffarnagar. As long as 1984 goes unpunished, there will be those who try to justify impunity elsewhere too.

For four decades, the victims of 1984 have lived in a quagmire where hopes of justice have been pulled down by the incessant delay in meting out this justice. They are seeking, as the elusive state calls it, a 'closure' that will help them go on with their lives. Not that they seek to forget what transpired or to stop grieving, but for the past thirty-nine years they have remained frozen in an unbearably horrific moment, and wish to find closure through the punishment of the perpetrators of 1984.

The screams of the victims of 1984 still echo in the narrow lanes of India, where thousands were butchered over three decades ago. It is time for India to ensure that the brutalities of 1984 and the years that followed do not remain a festering sore.

CHRONICLES OF THE KAURS

Some of the stories in this epilogue have been reproduced from various affidavits which I received through the Right to Information Act. In 2015, my Amnesty International team attempted to locate some of the women whose stories had come to light during the course of my research, but we were unable to do so. More than thirty years had passed since the pogrom of 1984, and many of these women and their families were no longer living at the addresses listed in the affidavits. However, these are vital stories, and to my mind, it is important that they are told rather than being left to gather dust in sarkari papers. As a long-time researcher, here is my homage to all the women who have been victims of violence, and my apologies to those whose tales I was unable to include.

PUNJAB

Harjeet Kaur

At nineteen years of age, Harjeet Kaur married Anar Singh Para, a lieutenant general in the Khalistan Liberation Force, on 16 February 1991. Tall and good-looking, Harjeet was very confident of her decision to marry Para. 'My decision was influenced by my

Epilogue

maternal uncle, Bakshish Singh Kaljug, and my mother's uncle, Giani Mor Singh. Uncle Mor Singh was a Hindu who had converted to Sikhism. He and his entire family had been killed in the Golden Temple during Operation Blue Star. They had strapped grenades to their bodies and dashed towards the army assault team's leading tank, jumping overboard and blowing it to bits.

'I was only twelve years old when the Akal Takht was attacked. In those days, my entire family used to talk about the movement and what had transpired in 1984. They all supported the movement. That's when I made the decision to become a kharku as well.

'I used to tell my uncle that I wanted to be a kharku but he always discouraged me. I never romanticized the concept of marriage, but when the time came for me to enter a matrimonial union, I made it clear to my family that I would only marry a kharku and no one else because I wanted to be a part of the movement. For me, this was the only way to join militant ranks.

'My wedding to Anar Singh Para was planned by my maternal uncle. My family didn't want me to marry Anar Singh but I told them that if they didn't let me marry him, I would flee and join the movement by myself. So, they consented, but my parents did not attend the wedding.

'My wedding took place in Baba Bakale in Amritsar late at night, with militants from five different factions in attendance. My wedding clothes were brought by Gurmukh Singh Nagoke's[7] wife. Everyone vanished in the dead of night, shortly after the wedding.

'While working for the movement, I resided with my husband in several areas across Punjab. It was my responsibility to deliver

Epilogue

arms and messages. I always used to carry a pistol with me for security.

'When I was pregnant, we relocated to Nanded, Hazoor Sahib, and my daughter was born there. But our happiness did not last long. In an orchestrated encounter, my husband was killed on 27 May 1992. At the time, my daughter was only fourteen days old. It had been just a day since I had left Nanded to go to Manmaar, where my husband was supposed to meet us. I was in Manmaar when I learned that he was dead.

'In that moment, I felt clueless about where I was going and what I was destined to do. I decided it would be best to join the supporters of the Khalistani movement. In the meantime, I moved in with my relatives in Punjab. But it wasn't for long.

'I was arrested at Harike, Tarn Taran, at my relatives' home. From there, I was taken to Mallanwalla in Ferozepur district and then to CIA Staff Tarn Taran, where I was held for six months.

'The CIA staff tortured me for days. I was even subjected to electric shocks, causing an incapacity to hear from one ear. Male police officers hurled abuses at me. A ghotna was put between my waist and knees, and a couple of officers stood on it, hitting my joints as they did so. To put it simply, the psychological torture was many times worse than the physical torture. For a while, my baby daughter was with me, but in time, she fell ill and was taken home by her grandmother.

'In December 1993, almost six months later, I was freed. But the police would come to my house at any time to rearrest or harass me, alleging that I could easily drift off the grid or pick up guns again. They even tried to force my family to get me married again, the incentive being my permanent freedom. For a while, I

Epilogue

refused, but then I eventually submitted to family pressure and married my dead husband's older brother, a man already married and a decade older than me. I stood bereft of a choice. I was staying with my in-laws, and while they were good people, they were also being regularly harassed by the police. After my elder brother was killed in a fake encounter, my mother was forced to leave our family home in the village with my ten-year-old brother. I had no roof to call my own, nor a house where I could go for shelter.'

⁓

From 1984 to 1989, Amnesty International was denied permission to enter Punjab to verify claims of human rights violations. Although Prime Minister Vishwanath Pratap Singh's National Front Coalition government announced in July 1990 that Amnesty International representatives could come to India for private visits or meetings with the government, before it could actually happen, the government was routed out of power in November 1990.

Amnesty International's report titled 'Human Rights Violations in Punjab: Use and Abuse of the Law' documented several stories of human rights violations across the state. During the late 1980s and the 1990s, women in Punjab were regularly detained and tortured either to force them to reveal information about their male relatives suspected of being militants or to prevent them from feeding or sheltering militants.

Amnesty's report highlighted the cases of Gurmeet Kaur, Gurdev Kaur and Sonia,[8] which were emblematic of the patterns of violence that women suffered in Punjab.

Epilogue

On 21 August 1989, an assistant superintendent of police (ASP) and six men in civilian clothes detained Gurmeet Kaur and Gurdev Kaur, both women in their thirties, from their workplace in Amritsar, in front of their colleagues. They were then driven to Batala's Beeco interrogation centre without any charges, except that their husbands were accused of having ties to Sikh militants.

Gurdev Kaur was released the following day on 22 August. In an interview published in the *Illustrated Weekly* on 24 September 1989, she detailed how she was tortured by senior police officers:

> He kept on hitting me while I screamed for mercy. He hit me so violently that the ligaments of my left arm and shoulder were torn. I fainted because it was so painful. When I regained consciousness, I heard the SSP (senior superintendent of police) telling an inspector, who was there to beat me, to hit me on the head. They then tied my hands behind and made me lie on the floor on my stomach. I was lashed with a whip and then interrogated about my husband. They placed planks on my legs and three men stood on it and rolled them over.[9]

Gurmeet Kaur's husband, Mehal Singh, is the elder brother of Sukhdev Singh, who was the head of Babbar Khalsa, an armed separatist organization. Gurmeet Kaur had not heard from her husband in five years, but she was still held in custody till 3 September 1989. She said that the police tortured her, and threatened to murder her and her children if she did not give up her husband's location. She revealed the truth of her torture in an

Epilogue

interview published in *The Times of India*, Patna, on 7 September 1989:

> I was hit constantly on my limbs, and chest ... After tying my hands, the senior police officer himself forcibly pushed me in order to make me lie down as I was unable to. As a result, I suffered an injury on my head as it hit against the ground. He meanwhile caught hold of a leather strap and began thrashing me. And whenever he felt tired there would be others to take over. This went on for days. Many times, I felt unconscious ... sometimes my torturers would be drunk and they would jeer and taunt me. Planks would be put on my thighs and four men would stand on them at a time. Sometimes they would threaten to force horse urine in my mouth. And once, they even took me out in a jeep saying that they were going to kill me.[10]

Sonia,[11] a native of Paili village in Hoshiarpur district, filed a complaint with the chief judicial magistrate of Hoshiarpur on 25 July 1989, alleging that four police officers from Hoshiarpur's Balachaur Police Station had unlawfully detained and gang raped her. The SHO, the Moharrir head constable and two additional head constables, all from the Balachaur Police Station, were reportedly implicated in the complaint.

On the morning of 9 February 1989, at around 5 a.m., four police officers had arrived at Sonia's house and questioned her about her cousin. When she was unable to offer any information, she was taken to Balachaur Police Station and detained. Sonia told Amnesty International that she was asked to sign a piece of blank paper. When she refused to do so, she was kicked and beaten by the station house officer and the head constable. She stated that the two men returned to her room at midnight on 9 February and raped her. Later that same night, she was also raped by two other head constables. She further stated that the SHO threatened to charge her with a crime or kill her if she told anyone about the rape.

The next day, on 10 February, Sonia was released. She said that after her release, senior medical officers at the civil hospitals in Balachaur and Garhshankar refused to examine her because they feared reprisal from the local police.[12]

According to a report released by Citizens for Democracy,[13] titled 'Report to the Nation, Oppression in Punjab'[14] and published in 1985, the house of Swaran Kaur, the fifty-year-old wife of ex-MLA Harbans Singh Ghuman of Ghumankala village, was raided forty-five times by the Indian Army, BSF and the police. Each time they came, they destroyed everything, including the furniture and bartan (utensils). They would mix different types of cereals with rice and they took away her tractor and servants.

They would show up at any moment, enter her room, wake up her sleeping children, grab her by the throat and force her to stand in the sun for hours—despite the fact that she had high blood pressure—until she passed out. Two of her four sons were imprisoned in Jodhpur; the youngest, a student, had gone to the Golden Temple on the 3 June to make a vow in connection with a college exam, and the other had gone to spend the night there till the stores reopened, when he could purchase some implements and tools for his farm. The third son was pounced upon and literally lifted and taken to CIA Staff Batala from the

Epilogue

bus stand. He was coming from the doctor, who was treating his child from polio; he was waiting with his wife and the sick child. He underwent inhumane torture.

Women in Punjab faced attacks from various quarters. Some were targeted by police and some were targeted by separatist groups. They were attacked for engaging in activities like selling tobacco, or being suspected of being police informants and, in many cases, they were called bad influences and loose-charactered women.[15]

~

Master Tara Singh's[16] daughter Rajinder Kaur was a prominent Sikh activist and a member of Parliament who defended and assisted many innocent Sikhs and activists detained following Operation Blue Star. She was killed by Sikh militants on 2 February 1989.

In Punjab, many innocent people became the target of both state and non-state actors, with members of armed secessionist groups killing hundreds of police officers, state officials and politicians, as well as members of rival Sikh groups and numerous Hindus and Sikhs, sometimes while holding them hostage. Furthermore, they have assassinated journalists and editors for what they have written or for refusing to write in the manner or language dictated by Sikh groups. They also assassinated two members of the judiciary in December 1990 alone. Punjab witnessed a surge in targeted assassinations, bombings and clashes between different militant groups. The atmosphere was fraught with fear and uncertainty as violence and instability was plaguing the region. Punjab is also an example of how unbridled discretionary powers

Epilogue

given to an institution or any office, especially the police force, can be catastrophic.

Kuljit Kaur

Kuljit Kaur Wariana, a tall and confident twenty-year-old woman, married Resham Singh Wariah Babbar, a Sikh militant, in 1988. Resham was a known extremist who had picked up arms after seeing the devastation left behind at Darbar Sahib in the wake of Operation Blue Star.

'I was aware of what I was getting into because my entire family actively participated in the movement. My sister was married to Mohinder Singh Mehta, one of Sant Jarnail Singh Bhindranwale's bodyguards. We revered Sant Bhindranwale; there was so much love for him. My wedding took place in the dark, in the presence of Baba Nanda Singh and Amarjeet Singh. We were unable to have a wedding in the daytime because of the threat of police raids. Following my marriage, I worked continuously for the movement, whether it was day or night. Our entire lives were dedicated to it.

'We were always on the move. One day, about two months after our wedding, we found ourselves resting near the motor (a water pump at the field) outside Meharhana village. I was bathing when suddenly the CRPF and Punjab Police surrounded us. Bullets started flying, and the men managed to escape through the main road. Unfortunately, I couldn't run because I was in the middle of my bath. I told my husband that I would go back to the village where we had stored our ammunition.' When I somehow managed to reach the safe house, the CRPF and Punjab Police were hot on my heels. I was left with little choice but to hide whatever I could.

Epilogue

With no female cop present, about half a dozen CRPF officers began assaulting me in one of the rooms. They didn't find what they were looking for, but they were happy enough to have caught me and to have discovered numerous firearms as well.

'When the CRPF asked me about my husband, his family and about the contact details of the other men, I told them, "Yes, I am his wife, but I don't know anything. I have been waiting here for him for months." My husband had warned me not to tell the police the truth. They took me from Meharhana to Fatehabad Chowki, where the Haryana Police from Pehowa arrived and interrogated me for hours.

'I was taken to Sarhali thana in Tarn Taran the next day, where I was probed every day by SSP Baldev Singh and Makhan Jalad, who used to humiliate and torture me. As before, I was questioned in the absence of a female police officer. They tortured me for eight days with the ghotna, with waterboarding, then by rolling a large wooden log on my thighs while three police officers either stood or sat atop it and by pulling off my nails. They also stretched my legs wider than 180 degrees.

'I can't tell you the kind of things they used to do and the names they used to call me. It was more difficult to endure the psychological torture than the physical one. Most times, the officers who tortured me were in a state of inebriation. Moreover, I was pregnant again at that time. The officers injected something into me and I suffered a miscarriage. Looking back, I can only say that it was murder. The officers showed me photographs of my wedding and the militants in attendance. But I refused to tell them anything.

'After running out of tactics to break me psychologically and physically, they took me to Harike, where they tried to entice

Epilogue

me with promises of money, a house, a car and a bodyguard, all in exchange for my aid in finding the men on their radar. They promised, "If you support us, we will defend you."

'I refused to tell them anything. Today, I feel proud of my decision, my decision to not tell them about our former residences and the names of the people who helped us. I knew there was nothing beyond torture that they could subject me to, so I kept quiet.

'One of the staff members at the Sarhali Police Station, who was well-known, informed my father that I had been arrested. I also requested him to inform my father of my statement. As expected, within days, my father was arrested and brought to the Mal Mandi Police Station in Amritsar. Fortunately, our statements matched and he was let off.

'The police then presented me before a magistrate in Patti to demand an extended remand but the magistrate refused to give any further remand orders. My body was bruised with visible marks. I was bleeding and barely able to stand on my own. The magistrate informed them that I was unfit for remand. The police then brought me back to Harike, from where I was transferred to the Gumtala jail in Amritsar, where I was kept for fifteen months. It was during my stint in jail that I learned that I had become a widow. I pleaded with the superintendent to allow me to meet my family. The next day, my sister and cousins visited me in jail. I refused to believe the story of my husband's death even though my mother told me that she had been at his cremation and had witnessed it with her own eyes.

'I made every effort to attend my husband's final rites but I was denied permission, something I will regret for the rest of my life. He was killed on 29 October 1999.

Epilogue

'I was given bail eight months after my husband's death, but the police arrived even before I could get home. They were curious about my future plans. I informed them that I would return to my in-laws' house.'

During the peak of militancy, the Punjab Police often coerced young women into remarriage, exerting pressure on their families to facilitate the marriage upon the death of their husbands or if these girls had taken up arms. Their strategy perhaps was rooted in the belief that once these women were married off, they would become preoccupied with their marital responsibilities and would be diverted from the involvement in militant activities. This manipulation of marriage was blatant exploitation, illustrating how police used societal norms as a tool to suppress women's agency and autonomy, overlooking the possibility that these women may have had no inclination towards militancy in the first place. They were merely married to men who were involved in militancy and they themselves had no role in it.

'I was asked to go to the police station every day to mark my attendance, but then the sarpanch of our village intervened and these visits stopped.

'I don't have a single regret nor do I believe that we did anything wrong. What they had done to our holy shrine makes my blood boil even now.

'I was not acquitted, but my case was dismissed.'

Sumanpreet Kaur

A teenager during Operation Blue Star, Sumanpreet Kaur calls herself a child of 1984. 'We were visiting the Golden Temple

Epilogue

in Amritsar in the summer of 1984, while my father was stationed there as an engineer with the Central Public Works Department (CPWD). Our family is originally from Delhi, but we were based in Patiala. We were in one of the rooms at the Parikrama when I saw men with firearms walking through it for the first time. A leader marched at the forefront, setting a brisk pace, while armed men followed closely behind, encircled by curious onlookers. This was very new to a teenager like me. It scared me.

'My mother took us to see Sant Jarnail Singh Bhindranwale at his daily assembly above the Langar Hall on our second day at the Golden Temple. I wondered why she had brought us there where armed men were roaming around the complex.

'My mother was completely enthralled with Sant Jarnail Singh Bhindranwale. When we arrived, no one stopped us or asked us any questions, as is customary at many other places when you meet notable figures. Everyone was welcome. We sat in the front row, and this was the first time that I met Sant Jarnail Singh Bhindranwale. He didn't smile or say anything to us, but he had a very steely expression on his face. Major General Shabeg Singh was also present.

'"All the weapons are pointing towards us," Sant Jarnail Singh Bhindranwale said, alluding to the paramilitary personnel who had assumed tactical positions surrounding the Golden Temple. In this, he was correct. Back then, there was no galleria around the Golden Temple. It was surrounded by private properties, most of which had been taken over by the state. Now when I think about it, I realize that occupying places like that can't be done without prior planning.

Epilogue

'At the time of Operation Blue Star, we were in Jaipur. We only returned to Punjab when things had calmed down. At the time, Punjab was literally cut off from the rest of the world. My father was on duty, and the civil administration later asked him to lead the clean-up work at the Golden Temple. But he was too horrified by the whole thing. Perhaps he had witnessed the gore left behind after Operation Blue Star. Devastated, he asked to be transferred out of the state. He never spoke about it, and he still gets uncomfortable if he is asked about it. Till date, he carries a half-burnt ang of the Guru Granth Sahib which he picked up from the complex all those years ago.

'I was saddened by the assassination of Prime Minister Indira Gandhi. For me, she was a woman who had overcome the glass ceiling in her professional life. It was inspiring to think about. But as events unfolded after that, I realized how drastically the lives of Sikh women had been altered. Sikh women in Delhi lost everything and those in Punjab had horrible experiences at the hands of the police.

'My maternal family was in Delhi when the violence broke out, and we were all frightened about my mamaji's family. We were glued to the phone, calling everyone we could think of to see whether my maternal family was safe. We were unable to communicate with them. There was a curfew in Patiala as well, but rumours of disaster had begun to circulate.

'On national television, our idol Amitabh Bachchan called for "*Khoon ka badla khoon se*! Blood will be avenged with blood!"'

(Similarly, Jagdish Kaur, a key witness in the Sajjan Kumar case, also remembers watching a similar story on television.)[17]

Epilogue

'There is little doubt that our Hindu brethren in Delhi helped many beleaguered Sikh families, but the monstrosity unleashed in Delhi was nothing short of genocide. Following the violence in Delhi, I was always afraid that someone would cut my braid, and I was sometimes afraid to go to huge gatherings and even to the assemblies in school because of my fear of crowds. My sleep was disrupted and I started to have disturbing nightmares. I was perplexed about why they intended to kill and attack Sikhs. Fear had overwhelmed me, and all I could think about were my family in Delhi, and whether they would be safe in the future or not.

'My experience in college in Patiala was much more distressing. We would hear tales of young boys getting kidnapped every day, and most of them never returned home.

'Then there were people who colluded with the police and brought hell into the lives of the women in Punjab. I was regularly hounded by the son of a high-ranking police official, who would follow me in a government vehicle with four commandos. He would occasionally stop me in the middle of nowhere. Every day, these men would taunt and harass ladies, but we couldn't intervene because we had nowhere to go. Punjab had become a police state by that time. When I reflect back, I believe we were still better, but what about the ladies who were not educated and who lived in rural Punjab where the police were treated as gods?

'I got married in 1991 and relocated to the United States of America. My parents were relieved since they had been worried about my safety in Punjab. But my teenage years had been scarred by the violence in Punjab, and I grew up cognizant of the obvious markings of being a Sikh. I was no longer a child after the carnage in Delhi.'

DELHI

Ajmer Kaur

Ajmer Kaur was twenty-five years old when her husband was killed in Sindhi Colony, New Delhi. They had recently shifted there and no one knew of them other than the colony's chowkidar.

'My Sardarji requested the mob by folding his hands, but they attacked Sardarji and knocked me out. When I regained consciousness, I saw my Sardarji on the ground, where the mob had set him ablaze with eucalyptus leaves and white powder. About ten members of the mob forbade us from approaching Sardarji.'

Mahesh Sharma

In his statement, Mahesh Sharma, thirty-four years old, stated that on 1 November 1984, he witnessed a mob carrying lathis, iron rods, oil cans and packets of white powder in Nimri Colony, Ashok Vihar. People were saying, '*Sardaron ko looto aur inko jaan se maaro*. Loot the Sardars and kill them.' First, the crowd ran towards the gurdwara and from there, they went to Quarter 617. The house was looted before it was set on fire, all while armed police officers stood nearby.

Mandadori Devi

In her statement, Mandadori Devi, wife of a police officer, said, 'On 1 November 1984, at around 3 p.m., the massacre began in Jahangirpuri When a mob came and repeatedly beat our

Epilogue

neighbours, my husband stepped out quickly to defend the victims. The mob demanded that my husband explain why he was protecting these people and that he step aside, but when he refused to do so, the mob assaulted him and beat him with a rod. He collapsed to the ground. The mobs were carrying a white powder that they were using to set their targets on fire.'

Updesh Kaur

'A mob attacked our colony on 1 November 1984 at around 11 a.m., and there were about 400 to 500 men. They were carrying lathis, iron rods, sticks, kerosene oil and some white powder with them. My husband had to hide because we saw that the houses of Sikhs were being looted and Sikhs were being put to death.

'On 2 November 1984, my husband went to the police station, but instead of filing his complaint, the police abused him and asked him to go away. He was killed by the mob right outside the police station. I was told by many that ex-MP Sajjan Kumar was there. The police acted like silent spectators and did nothing.'

Gurbachan Kaur

'"Where is your Bhindranwale? Bring him, and we will make your Khalistan now!" shouted the mob on 1 November 1984 at around 11 a.m. even as they threatened to abduct our girls. The railway line lies directly across from our house, and the train was packed when it arrived. When it came to a stop, those who disembarked from it were armed with lathis, pointed iron rods, chains, pitchforks and a white powder that ignited when thrown on anything.

'When the mob arrived at our block, our Muslim and Dalits neighbours appeared and whisked us away to their homes. They assured us that they were there to protect us and that nothing would harm us. When the mob arrived at the house where we were hiding, the men threatened to burn it down unless the owner turned us in.

'A few other Sikh lads had been hidden by some Hindu neighbours, but a lawyer alerted the mob about them. The mob then struck down the door and entered the house. They discovered the lads hiding under some beds inside and attacked them with rods before setting them on fire with the white powder.

'The mob was shouting that they would take away the Sikh women and make them their concubines. They said, "Their men are killed. They have to live with us now."

'When the women of Nangloi reached out to the police station, we were not allowed inside. "Go away, go away, you are Sikh bitches," we were told. The mob attacked my husband with iron rods and daggers and then burnt him with the white powder; men in the mob were wearing white rubber gloves. The mob was shouting, "We are creating Khalistan for the Sikhs!"'

Anek Kaur

'We first heard noises at 8 p.m. on 1 November 1984, and as we went up to our roof, we saw fires raging at multiple sites, with dense smoke spiralling out from the Nangloi side. We were afraid that something might happen, so we sought refuge with our neighbours.

Epilogue

Around 9 p.m., a strong and armed mob came and surrounded our houses. One of the mob's leaders, Rattan, pointed at our houses. Instead of halting the mob, the police were urging them to kill Sikhs and set fire to their homes. Rattan Singh was accompanied by the sons of Congress leader Jai Kishan, who was supplying petrol and holding a white powder that caught fire instantly when thrown on an object. SHO Bhatti threatened to shave our heads if we sought to report him. We were in E-6 when Congress MP Sajjan Kumar and Congress leader Jai Kishan came in a jeep. We ran towards them for help. But Jai Kishan said that in our village, we were the only Sikhs left. He said that he would get us killed by the villagers. Sajjan Kumar said that we should be beaten to death.'

Ghuddi Kaur

'On 1 November 1984, at about 7 a.m., a mob of tentatively a thousand people came to our doorstep. They tried to enter the house by breaking down our main door. Clueless of the developments, I ran to my husband. The mob broke down the door and caught hold of my husband. Two men from the mob overpowered me. My husband was carrying our son. The mob threw kerosene on my husband and set him on fire. My husband threw our child off himself to protect him from the flames. I extinguished the fire on my child with my dupatta.

'My husband was trying to run away, but they hit him with a barcha (spear) and a gandasa (axe) and killed him. My father and brother were also killed. We went to the mosque from there but the mob had already reached there and was threatening us from the outside.'

Epilogue

Param Kaur[18]

'At 2 a.m., our house's back wall was shattered. The owner of Satvir Hotel lives behind our house. He was attempting to enter our house through the back wall. Brahmanand and his three brothers threw kerosene oil on my house and set it on fire despite me pleading with them, with folded hands.

'My husband and two sons attempted to flee as the fire spread. While attempting to jump over the wall, my Sardar was shot by a bullet. From the road, SHO Bhatti was firing from the front. The gunshots also struck my sons.

'My sons, though hit, were gasping. Then, between 7–8 a.m. on 2 November 1984, they came and dragged my sons away. As I ran towards them, trying to help them, I was caught, stripped naked and raped by Nathu Pradhan and Gupta Brahmanand Ramesh. Nobody even gave me a dupatta to cover myself with as I ran naked on the roads.'

Teedee Kaur

'We were deeply saddened when we learned of Indira Gandhi's killing. On 1 November 1984, at about 9 p.m., the power went off and we all came out. A throng erupted, yelling "Indira Gandhi *ki jai*! *Khoon ka badla khoon*! Hail Indira Gandhi! Blood will be avenged with blood!" at the top of their lungs. These men were hiding behind masks. Some forced their way into our homes, dragging women and children away.

'They were yelling, "Come out quickly or we'll burn you alive." We were escorted to a nearby park. Swords, knives and white

Epilogue

powder were among the weapons carried by the mob. My son was beaten by the mob and my house was set on fire. My son lay inside the burning house. The next day when we arrived home, I saw some watery discharge oozing from his half-burnt body parts. My daughter's wedding items, including her clothes, cash and a sewing machine, were all stolen.'

Manya Kaur[19]

'My husband was killed on 3 November 1984 at about 4 a.m. I cried a lot. I was pregnant at that time. Ram Niwas threatened to hit my stomach and kill my unborn child. Our relatives, three of them, were visiting us and were also killed. Ram Niwas, Satvir and Kala tried to molest me. I along with other women of Mangolpuri kept going to the police station for three days for help, but no one bothered.'

Slawati Kaur

'I was stabbed in the thigh with a trishul (trident), and my brother was stabbed in the skull. The mob then asked if I had a pair of scissors, but all of our belongings had already been plundered, so I didn't have anything. Then a man arrived with a pair of scissors and cut my brother's hair. The mob then carried him away. I hid inside someone's house for the night. The next day, I noticed that sweepers were loading bodies into trucks.'

Swaran Kaur

'On 1 November 1984, at about 10 a.m., from the terrace of our house we noticed smoke streaming from the entire Mayapuri area.

Around 12 p.m., some 100 to 500 people carrying lathis and iron rods passed us while on their way to the DTC bus stand. A vehicle was accompanying the mob, and it was loaded with supplies of oil. It came to a halt in front of our store. When the locals arrived, the mob dispersed from outside our shop.

'Fateh Nagar and Shiv Nagar's Hindus and Sikhs banded together and decided that nothing would happen in their neighbourhoods. To prevent intruders from entering, the Hindus and Sikhs built wards and guard stations along all major thoroughfares. My husband, an ex-military personnel, was giving a briefing on the nakabandhi (temporary check point) positions to everyone. When the cops arrived and instructed everybody to go back inside, they resisted. My husband assured the cops that the area was being guarded by both Hindus and Sikhs, and that we would not allow any kind of intimidation. But the police did not take this in the correct attitude.

'On 3 November 1984, the police arrived at our house, knocked and ordered us to open the door. Five or six officers entered our house forcibly, abusing me and my daughter-in-law. Then they dragged my husband to a jeep that was parked on the side of the road and began beating him with the butts of their pistols. I began screaming, "Please save my husband!" My husband was being carried away. I didn't let my two sons come out since they were on the roof, and had they come out, the cops would have taken them away as well.

'An advocate went to the police station on our behalf and he informed us that my husband had been charged under Section 307 of the Indian Penal Code (IPC).[20] We filed a bail application,

Epilogue

which was approved, but my husband was not released until 12 November 1984.

'I sent my sons to meet their father in jail, and my husband informed them that he had been beaten all the way to the police station in a vehicle. They promised to set him free if he killed two Sikhs with his licensed gun, but he refused.

'After arriving at the police station, the SHO handed him over to three or four officers who had previously beaten him. They punched his stomach so brutally that following his release, he complained of a pain in his stomach all the time. He died on 13 June 1985.'

Gurjeet Kaur[21]

'Not even three dupattas are enough to wipe our tears ... Nobody was spared, neither old women nor little girls. There was no one we could call. All the men in our colony had been burnt alive only that morning—all 500 of them—even as the women begged to be spared from molestation. Their attackers demanded to know why they were being bashful and warned that if they tried to run away, their breasts would be cut off.'[22]

Pritam Kaur

'My sons and husband were dragged out of our home in Kabir Basti and were burnt alive in front of me. I was forced to watch this unbearable sight. I know all the assailants very well, but I couldn't name them initially; I was too scared. I remember standing there, crying. I pleaded with the police constable present there, but he slapped me and started hurling abuses and said that the Sikhs are

Epilogue

traitors. The SHO of the Subzi Mandi Police Station, Jai Bhagwan Malik, and ACP Raghubir Singh were present along with armed police personnel. When my husband and son were engulfed in fire, the officers were shouting that all the Sikhs should be killed and not one should be spared.'

Nanki

'On 1 November 1984, at the Gokalpuri Chowki, I witnessed Sikh men being burnt alive. They were crying in pain while the crowd was chanting, "They are doing the bhangra now." To reach home, I had to jump over a number of dead bodies that lay lined on the road. I saw police officers dragging Sikh truck drivers out of their vehicles in Bhajanpura before beating them brutally and then burning them with their trucks. I was unable to reach my home because of the mob around it. I saw Kiran,[23] a woman from the neighbourhood, struggling in pain on the ground. She had been raped by eight or ten men. They doused her in kerosene, placed cots on top of her and then set her ablaze.

'My husband was first attacked with iron rods, and then someone took kerosene from my house and poured it on him. I pleaded with them but they were unmoved. I couldn't do anything. I begged the assailants to kill me as well. The mob was instigated by Jamna Devi.'

Partap Kaur

'On 31 October 1984, I was on night duty. Sikhs were being slaughtered in buses and autos, according to the reports. I skipped out on my responsibilities in order to return home. On my way

EPILOGUE

home, I visited the homes of our Sikh neighbours to advise them not to ride their scooters since Sikhs were being slain. When I told my brother about it, he reprimanded me, saying that we were all pucca Congressmen and there was nothing to worry about. In fact, when he heard of Mrs Gandhi's death, he struck his head against the wall in grief. On 1 November 1984, at about 10.30 a.m., around thirteen or fourteen men dressed in white clothes and riding on cycles and motorcycles, were heard shouting, "Kill the Sikhs and burn their houses after looting them. For three days, we are the rulers!"'

Banso Kaur[24]

'On 1 November 1984, the police came to our house and told us that unless we hid inside our houses, they would kill us. On 2 November 1984, at around 7 or 8 a.m., a mob of some four to five thousand people broke down our door and violently entered our home. My husband was attacked and the mob bound me by my legs and hands. Along with my three-month-old daughter, I was forced to watch the gruesome sight of my husband being burnt alive.

'A police officer named Bhatti was also there. My husband had been in Iraq for five years, and all the goods he had brought back from Iraq—a tape recorder, blankets, a radio and some clothing—were stolen. I was forced to stay in Lal Kothi with my husband's killers, I knew all of them.'

Gulbano Kaur

'We were frightened. The police ordered us to go inside our homes. Soon, the mob attacked and the police were mere bystanders. The mob was armed and I knew some of them. One of them fired a bullet at my husband. When I went to my husband's aid, they fired bullets at me too. I managed to carry my injured husband to my house with the help of my neighbour, but the mob followed us. We spent a night at our neighbour's home. On 2 November 1984, when we came out, many people taunted us by saying, "Go to the police, they will save you." I know all of the men who burnt my husband alive.'

Tilak Vihar: The Widows' Colony

Shanti Kaur's husband and brother-in-law were put to death with swords. 'My brother-in-law was lying with his stomach cut open. God is a witness to my pain. We were begging for water. The images of the atrocities committed in 1984 haunt me even today.'

Lakhbir Kaur's[25] husband, five of her brothers and a few other relatives were killed during the 1984 massacre. 'They put a tyre filled with petrol around my husband's neck and set it on fire outside a police station. A middle-aged man from the mob came back at night and tried to touch me inappropriately. When I resisted, he went out and called his entire group. They searched my house and killed all the remaining men from my family who had been hiding inside. I was regularly threatened and harassed, so I decided to withdraw my case. I was scared to pursue it. The government should come and see how we are living.'

Hukumi Kaur lost her husband, brother-in-law, father-in-law and eleven other relatives. 'The men from my family were burnt alive at the main door of our house. My husband was killed three days later; his eyes were gouged out and he was burnt alive. It's been thirty-six years with no justice whatsoever. We are helpless.'

Sundari Kaur lost her husband and other family members. 'My husband was an autorickshaw driver. He was killed outside somewhere. I didn't even see his dead body. We only found his burnt auto at the police station. I am still suffering from the pain of 1984. Justice isn't anywhere close. They looted everything we had, and we were left to rot and die with nothing.'

Amarjeet Kaur lost her husband and her brother-in-law. 'My husband and his brother were killed in Badli. They were burnt alive by a mob of hundreds. The mob was throwing some white powder which immediately caught fire and even exploded. We are the forgotten citizens of India.'

Operation Woodrose

As word of Operation Blue Star spread, there was a massive public backlash. Though Darbar Sahib, the sanctum sanctorum within the Golden Temple, remained unharmed, the Akal Takht had been irreparably damaged. The army began patrolling the Punjab countryside looking for suspected terrorists, ostensibly in order to avert public unrest from erupting. Operation Woodrose was the name of this drill. When a large number of villagers from Amritsar's border area began heading towards the Golden Temple, the army and the paramilitary forces intervened and halted them. But the Sikhs were angry. They said they were following Sant Bhindranwale's call, 'If any attack befalls the Golden Temple, it's the duty of every Sikh to be ready for sacrifice and come to the Golden Temple.'

Epilogue

The impact of Operation Blue Star on Sikh soldiers within the Indian Army was particularly devastating. There were reports of collective insubordination involving around 3,000 deserters in roughly a dozen army units, beginning with the 9 Sikh Regiment. For some time, these incidents threw the army's fundamental ethos into disarray, while many deserters were court-martialled and removed from service.

The government detained a number of politicians and outlawed the All India Sikh Students Federation. Furthermore, the Indian Army undertook operations in the countryside, during which hundreds of Sikhs, mostly young men, were held for questioning and, in many cases, tortured or killed.

For maintaining the legality of Operation Woodrose, Punjab and Chandigarh were declared 'disturbed areas' by the Government of India under the Punjab-Chandigarh Disturbed Area Act of 1983. Additionally, the army was given unprecedented powers to detain and arrest civilians through the enactment of the Armed Forces (Punjab and Chandigarh) Act of 1983.

On 5 June 1984, Kulbir Singh, a diminutive man with a long beard, who ran an X-ray clinic in Gurdaspur, was detained at a local market where he had gone to grab some groceries.

'On 4 June 1984, DIG Pritam Singh Bhinder contacted my uncle, the president of Gurdwara Singh Sabha, Gurdaspur, and informed him that a curfew would be enforced at 4 p.m. He told my uncle to inform the gurdwara that there would be no evening prayers. There was no connection with the outside world, and the only news we had access to was through the BBC's radio channel.

'The next day, I went out to buy groceries because there was no food at home and the stores had been instructed to close down

Epilogue

when the curfew began. Nobody knew how long it was going to take. I had no idea that the army was waiting for me outside. There were two army vehicles waiting for me, and the moment I stepped out, I was surrounded by jawans. There were two officials, Major Khosan and Subedar Hari Singh, who was from Gurdaspur.'

Major Khosan motioned for Kulbir Singh to step forward and raise his hands. They then drove Kulbir to his house and searched it thoroughly.

'The army searched my house and looked everywhere, including the cowshed. They were looking for evidence against me. The army recovered two licensed guns, one revolver and one double-barrelled gun from my home. I was fortunate that Major Khosan gave a recovery receipt to my family, which is also the reason I am alive today.'

When the army did not find anything, they detained Kulbir. 'They brought me from my house to the army camp, adjacent to the Railway Road, at about noon. They did not misbehave with me or say anything initially. But they asked if I wanted some food. They were friendly for some time, but things changed soon. Major Khosan, Subedar Hari Singh and some other officials forced me to sit in a vehicle. Then they removed my turban, tied my hands with a rope and covered my eyes. Everything would be all right, Subedar Hari Singh assured me. He told me to be patient because the Sikh community was under a great deal of strain. They then took me to Batala's Baring College.'

After a few hours in Baring College, Kulbir was asked to sit in another truck. 'There were two trucks, one of which was travelling ahead of us. After an hour on the road, both the vehicles came to a halt and I was told to get down. My eyes were covered by the

Epilogue

fabric, but if I moved my neck backwards, I could see a little bit. The jawans were making everyone stand in a line. But when they came to me, Major Khosan shouted, "You motherfuckers, we can't shoot him. We've picked him up from his house and handed over the recovery receipts." After two or three minutes, they began firing, and I could hear bullets striking the heads and chests of those around me. I'll never forget those sounds; it sounded like someone was puncturing a liquid bag with a needle, but these were real people, and those shouts of helplessness still resonate in my ears. There was a deafening silence after a few minutes. I was sure we stopped at some bridge, but I'm not sure where.'

Kulbir was ordered to sit in a truck and was taken to the kotwali close to the Golden Temple, and from there, he was sent to Clock Tower Square at around 5 p.m.

'At the kotwali, I saw some prominent faces including Jathedar Vedanti, Jasbir Singh Ghuman and Harminder Sandhu (General Secretary, All India Sikh Student Federation) and an injured Pritam Kaur Bariar, wife of Rachpal Singh. Harminder Sandhu asked me what position I had been manning. I told him that I had been picked up from my house in Gurdaspur.

'We were transported like animals to Sainik School on Atari Road on 6 June 1984, at around 7 p.m. It was a hot summer evening and we didn't have access to water or fans. Because each room had so many people in it, it became claustrophobic, and people began to pass out. Some wounded Sikh young men, who were already present in the rooms when we got there, died in front of us because there was no medical assistance available for us. People were actually dying of thirst; some had gone three days without any water. I drank water from the latrine tap. Everyone there was

Epilogue

terrified for their lives. They took our turbans away and gave us a small piece of cloth to cover our heads. I was in the same clothes from 8 June to 24 June. The army began screening us on 9 June, and they used to call everyone for interrogation twice a day.

'They would summon us to a room separated by a curtain, where men were instructed to sit on a stool in front of the curtain, and then someone on the other side of the curtain would talk in a thick Punjabi accent and inquire about various things. They would ask the same thirty or forty questions every day, and this went on for a few days.

'Oye! Do you know me? What's your name? Who are your friends with? Why are you here?'

Kulbir learned afterwards that behind the curtains were Punjabi police officers, including the SHO from Gurdaspur.

'I was summoned again on the night of 18 June. My eyes were covered with a thick black cloth. The army officials told me to sit in a truck. I was sweating and I was afraid they were going to kill me that night. When they didn't stop after a few hours on the road, my anxiety grew, and when they finally did stop, I believed that was it. I was mentally prepared to get killed. When I stepped down from the truck, I could tell that there were a number of other individuals as well. But they didn't kill me; I was taken to a government school in Gurdaspur and transferred to Dera Baba Nanak on 19 June 1984. I was taken for interrogation to city thana Dera Baba Nanak; the SHO (I won't identify him) was a very humble man, and they didn't do much.

'The SHO was a devout Sikh man who told me that when the army officers' duty changed, I could go take a bath. Taking a bath felt like a treat as well. The SHO told me that the curfew would

Epilogue

be relaxed at 4 p.m. and that there would be a lot of locals present then, so he could pass on my message to my family. However, he made it plain that I was not to tell anyone about our talk.'

Kulbir sent a message to the radiographer at Dera Baba Nanak's civil hospital; the man was a buddy and Kulbir was sure he would help. But the radiographer's leg was fractured and he was unable to help. However, he passed Kulbir's message to his friends in Gurdaspur. Finally, Kulbir's father, along with his friend and advocate Balkar Singh, came to see him on 20 June. They brought food and clothing with them, but they were not allowed to give anything to Kulbir.

'Every hour, the army would check on me to see if I had changed my clothes or anything. I did change into my white underwear, but no one seemed to notice. On the night of 20 June, I was transferred again, first to Gurdaspur and then to Tibri, where guys in plain clothes told me that I would be released and given money, but that I would have to help them find other militants. They said that I would be safe if I did so. I didn't consent to anything. I had no knowledge of any militant's whereabouts. How could I have known any radicals when I am a moderate? I am a follower of the Akali leaders and our leader Harchand Singh was a non-violent man.

'They took me to the Qadian Police Station on the evening of 22 June. There were so many people from Gurdaspur at the station, including ex-MLA Master Jodh Singh.

'On June 23 at around 12 a.m., a group of army officials instructed me to wash my face and offered me some water before telling me that I would be released if I signed a document, which

Epilogue

I refused to do. I was sure they would kill me if I signed the document.

'At around 5 p.m., the army officials tied my hands together and forced me into a car, which they then abandoned on the side of a road at Buttar village. A farmer working in his field had seen everything. He called to me, and on seeing that I was still in my underwear, he gave me some clothes and some food. He told me that the curfew was in effect right then, but that it would be lifted at around 8 p.m. He then offered to drop me off near the Batala highway once the curfew lifted.'

Police and paramilitary forces in Punjab detained thousands of people without a warrant. The security forces making these arrests did not identify themselves, and the arrested individuals or their relatives were not informed of the reasons for these arrests or the specific charges brought against them. In many cases, these arrests were not even recorded in the police stations' daily registers.

Even when there were eyewitnesses to these unlawful arrests or detentions, the police refused to acknowledge that they detained people arrested in Punjab on suspicion of being members or sympathizers of Sikh armed groups advocating for a separate Sikh state. Such people were held in illegal detention for weeks, if not months, with no record either of their arrest or the location of their detention.

Thousands of cases involving the disappearance Sikh young men and women remain unsolved to this day.

Acknowledgements

This book would not have been possible without my family's tolerance and encouragement, especially my mother, as well as Amnesty International—the organization allowed me to broaden my views by putting me in command of a small team investigating the 1984 anti-Sikh atrocities. Without the help and cooperation of everyone I met and spoke with, this book would not have seen the light of day.

All the women survivors of the slaughter and the violence in Punjab, who spoke up like they'd never spoken out before and who shared their own stories. Nirpreet Kaur, Darshan Kaur, Jasmeet Kaur, Kulbir Kaur, Sitara, and all others, took time out of their busy schedules to assist me in gaining access to critical accounts. Nivedita Menon, with whom I initially discussed the idea behind this book. To all of them I owe a debt of thanks.

Acknowledgements

Uma Chakravarti was the first person I met when I began investigating the topic, and her ideas have helped me enhance the research. Several individuals counselled, reprimanded and corrected me during the course of my research and writing. I am grateful to Harminder Kaur who is not just a mentor but a motherly figure to me. She has been my greatest teacher about Punjab. I am thankful to Josy Joseph, Omair Ahmad and Prabhjot Singh for being my most steadfast guides.

I am grateful to Kuldip Nayar, who generously shared his insightful thoughts, and the late Justice Rajinder Sachar, whom I only met once at the launch of my report.

I am grateful to my team at Amnesty International, most importantly Sampurna Khasnabis, for going to the police station on a daily basis to get copies of the FIRs.

To Anand Mangnale, who has been a continuous supporter through everything, thank you for all the free coffee and for putting up with my shenanigans. Smriti Singh, for bringing amazing homecooked food every day for me.

To Karan, who accompanied me on research excursions and consented to be my cameraperson in the sweltering June heat. To Aman Joon, who accompanied me to Chandigarh and Mohali and recorded all of my interviews.

Thank you, Owais, Rahul and Ravi Bathla, for your unwavering support, especially Rahul, for standing by me during challenging times and putting up with my rage. And a heartfelt thank you to Sukhman Sandhu for introducing me to the residents of Gurdaspur.

Thank you, Rahil Mehta, for opening your home in both Amsterdam and Mumbai, and for encouraging me to pursue my writing endeavours. Your support means a lot.

Acknowledgements

Devjot, for always being there for me, whether it was procuring inexpensive hotel rooms for me to stay in or spending days with me on my research visits to Amritsar. To his mother, Surinder Kaur, who accommodated me by opening her kitchen at strange hours.

To the people in Punjab who have helped me in a variety of ways and who don't wish to be named. To all the protagonists of this book. To Ali Ahmad and Naryani Basu for their reactions to my early drafts. I am indebted to all of them.

I am grateful to my siblings Raman and Gagan, and to my sister-in-law Preeti and brother-in-law Perdeep Singh for their unwavering support. My nephews Vivasvat and Ajooni, and my niece Gurmehar, who would instantly brighten my day with their grins.

I owe this book to Kanishka, without whom it would not have been published. I would also like to thank my editor Swati Chopra and the team at HarperCollins India for their immense support and unwavering commitment to this project.

To my grandmother, Dhanwant Kaur, who walked miles during the Partition for safety, and to my grandfather, Rangil Singh, and uncle, Mohan Singh, who tragically lost their lives in a bomb blast in Jammu and Kashmir. Remembering my maternal grandfather, Gyan Singh, whose forward-thinking stories shaped my mother's beliefs and inspired her to pass that legacy on to me. Additionally, my aunt, Kulwant Kaur, would read stories to me from her Braille books.

I've been quite lucky in terms of my friends, who have helped me in a variety of ways. I want to thank all of them.

At last, to all the bullies in school, who have laughed at me, hit me and called me names.

Notes

INTRODUCTION

1 Foreword by Desmond Tutu in *Reconciliation after Violent Conflict*, handbook, published by International Institute for Democracy and Electoral Assistance, 2003.
2 *Who Are the Guilty*, PUDR/PUCL, 1984, p 64.

1. SAKA NEELA TARA—OPERATION BLUE STAR

1 The Akali Dal, officially known as the Shiromani Akali Dal (SAD), is a prominent regional political party in India, with a strong presence in the state of Punjab. Originating from the term 'Akali', meaning 'timeless' or 'eternal' in Punjabi, the party is closely associated with Sikh principles and has historically advocated for the interests of the Sikh community.

Notes

2   The Anandpur Sahib Resolution was a policy programme of the Shiromani Akali Dal, adopted by its working committee at Shri Anandpur Sahib on 16–17 October 1973. It aimed to secure greater autonomy for the state, protect Sikh identity and ensure a fair distribution of resources for Punjab.
3   As per Kanwar Dhami in *Dreams after Darkness* by Manraj Gill, the Akal Federation was the most silent and invisible group, for it was based on the principle of wresting power through political propaganda.
4   Akhand Kirtani Jatha is a collection of Sikhs who believe in living life the way Sikh Gurus have instructed.
5   *Blue Star over Amritsar: The Real Story of June 1984*, Harminder Kaur, Corporate Vision, 2006, p. 10.
6   A Jathedar, esteemed as a leader, is selected to preside over and maintain discipline within a Jatha, which is a collective body of Sikhs.
7   Copy of a letter dated 2 June 1984 that Gurcharan Singh Tohra wrote to the prime minister of India.
8   *Blue Star over Amritsar*, Harminder Kaur, p. 11.
9   Giani Kirpal Singh's Eyewitness Account of Operation Blue Star, Anurag Singh, B. Chattar Singh Jiwan Singh, 1993, pp. 2–3.
10 White paper on Punjab's agitation 10 July 1984.
11 Ibid.
12 'Sacrificing Sikhs: The Need for an Investigation', Sikh Federation (UK), 2017.
13 'Margaret Thatcher Gave Full Support over Golden Temple Raid, Letter Shows', *The Guardian*, 15 January 2014; https://www.theguardian.com/world/2014/jan/15/margaret-thatcher-golden-temple-raid-support-letter
14 'The Untold Story before Operation Bluestar', *India Today*, 30 November 1999; https://www.indiatoday.in/magazine/the-big-

NOTES

story/story/20140210-operation-bluestar-indira-gandhi-singh-bhindranwale-army-800031-1999-11-29

15 Jallianwala Bagh is a park close to the Golden Temple where hundreds of unarmed people were massacred by British General Reginald Dyer on the day of baisakhi, 13 April 1919. Amidst the charged atmosphere of anti-British sentiments, the tranquil Jallianwala Bagh in Amritsar transformed into the haunting stage of a tragic episode. The crowd, gathering on Baisakhi Day to peacefully protest against the repressive Rowlatt Act, soon faced the unthinkable. Brigadier General Reginald Dyer, leading British troops in Amritsar, issued a ruthless order that forever altered the destiny of those present. Without warning or avenues for escape, the soldiers unleashed a hail of bullets upon the unsuspecting crowd, firing approximately 1,650 rounds for a harrowing ten minutes. The casualties, estimated conservatively at 379 lives lost and over a thousand wounded, represented a brutal turning point in India's struggle for independence. Dyer's intent to instil fear and awe reverberated in the aftermath, sparking outrage and solidarity among Indians against British rule. The Jallianwala Bagh massacre, etched in history, served as a poignant reminder of the sacrifices endured on the path to India's eventual liberation.
16 The hostel complex within the Golden Temple premises houses the Teja Singh Samundri Hall, SGPC office, Guru Nanak Niwas and various sarais.
17 The Damdami Taksal is a Sikh seminary or school that was founded by the tenth Sikh guru, Sri Guru Gobind Singh Ji.
18 Granthi is a ceremonial reader of Shri Guru Granth Sahib.
19 Satwant Kaur video interview with Sangat TV in 2011.
20 *Operation Blue Star: True Story*, K.S. Brar, UBS Publishers, 2003, pp. 70, 71.
21 Pritam Kaur's interview to Safar TV.

22 Ibid.
23 Toshakhana is generally associated with a treasury or storage place for valuable items.
24 *Blood on Green, Punjab's Tryst with Terror*, P.P.S. Gill., Bookwell Publications, 2017, pp. 5, 6.
25 *Blue Star over Amritsar*, Harminder Kaur, p. 51.
26 *Oppression in Punjab*, Hind Mazdoor Kisan Panchayat, 1985, p. 75.

2. CHAURASI KI NA INSAFI

1 *Indira: India's Most Powerful Prime Minister,* Sagrika Ghose, Juggernaut Books, 2017, p. 5.
2 *Never Ever We Forget Our Martyrs: A Commemorative Volume on the Occasion of the 30th Anniversary of Sikh Genocide of November 1984*, The Sikh Forum, November 2014.
3 For the protection of her privacy, the name of the survivor has been changed.
4 'Essay on Carnage', The Sikh Forum, 2014.

3. SULTANPURI

1 For the protection of her privacy, the name of the survivor has been changed.

4. RAJ NAGAR

1 Sajjan Kumar is one of the prime accused in the 1984 Sikh massacre and is in jail serving a life term.

6. HONDH

1 Cluster of farmhouses.

NOTES

7. NOVEMBER 1984

1 *Blue Star over Amritsar*, p. 112.
2 The deficiencies in media coverage of communal violence, particularly when the majority inflicts atrocities on minorities, bring to light a reality that is frequently concealed by the claims of journalistic objectivity. In actuality, choices made by journalists regarding what to publish have never been completely unrestrained. Instead, these decisions are consistently shaped by the prevailing values and cultural norms of the society in which they operate. Journalists navigate a complex landscape where societal influences play a pivotal role in determining the narratives that find their way into the public domain, challenging the notion of absolute journalistic impartiality.
3 Lubanki, also known as Labanki, is an Indo-Aryan language that was once spoken by the Labana tribe in the Punjab region. This dialect, which is now extinct among the Labanas of Punjab, was a blend of Marwari, Saraiki, Gujarati and Marathi influences. However, Rajasthani Labanas continue to use and speak this dialect.
4 Swami Agnivesh was an Indian social activist, politician and advocate for human rights and social justice.
5 Nagrik Ekta Manch was a citizen unity forum formed to promote solidarity and provide assistance to the Sikh community affected by the violence.

8. FROM PENS TO GUNS

1 Khalistan Commando Force is a militant organization.

9. MILITANT BRIDE

1 'Kharku' literally translates to 'courageous'. It is a self-designated Punjabi term for Sikh militants.

NOTES

2   Former Congress member of Parliament, Sajjan Kumar has been acquitted in a case linked to the murder of seven individuals from the Sikh community during the 1984 massacre in the Sultanpuri area. However, he will continue to serve his sentence in Tihar Jail, as he was handed a life imprisonment verdict by the Delhi High Court in 2018 for his involvement in another case. This case pertains to the killing of five Sikhs in Raj Nagar Part I in Palam Colony on 1–2 November, 1984, as well as the arson attack on a gurdwara in Raj Nagar.

10. THE DAUGHTER OF A COP

1. Vrinda Grover is a lawyer, researcher and human rights and women's rights activist based in New Delhi, India.
2. Bhindranwale Tiger Force of Khalistan was a militant outfit, now defunct.
3. PTC Punjabi is a Punjabi television network headquartered in Mohali, Punjab.
4. Sant Nirankari mission is a spiritual organization based in Delhi.
5. Khalistan Liberation Force is a separatist organization.
6. Reht maryada is a Sikh code of conduct, which is a set of rules outlining the responsibilities and the proper practices for Sikhs.
7. Operation Black Thunder 2 was a military operation conducted in India, targeting militants within the Golden Temple complex in Amritsar, Punjab.
8. Babbar Khalsa is a millitant organization.
9. Those who were once militant or Khalistani sympathizers, but later became informers and assisted the police in their quest for militants are referred to as sarkari cats.
10. Interestingly, and perhaps significantly, many like Jasmeet believe that the CATS were the ones who deliberately sabotaged the Khalistan movement, leading to public antagonism against a movement that she herself took great pride in back in the day.

NOTES

11. LETTERS FROM JAIL

1. Akhand Kirtani Jatha is a collection of Sikhs who believe in living the life Sikh Gurus have instructed.
2. The Damdami Taksal is a Sikh seminary or school that was founded by the tenth Sikh Guru, Sri Guru Gobind Singh Ji.
3. For the protection of privacy, the name of the survivor has been changed.
4. Asia Watch Report, 1990, Patricia Gossman.
5. *Dreams after Darkness*, Manraj Garewal, Rupa Publications, 2004.
6. Kulbir was hesitant to admit this.
7. Halt the Hate Project was a tracker to record hate crimes in India.
8. Some victims had the ghotna placed behind their knees after which their legs were flexed over it. But the most common method was for the ghotna to be rolled slowly down the thighs or the hips till the calves, with one or more of the heaviest policemen standing on it while the victims lay prone. This form of torture left no scars. Extensive bruising and the inability to walk were the primary results, and even years afterwards, victims frequently experienced discomfort while walking long distances.
9. For the protection of privacy, the name of the survivor has been changed.
10. Gurbachan Singh Manochahal was a Sikh militant and founder of Bhindranwale Tiger Force of Khalistan.

12. WIDOWS IN DELHI

1. Gurmukh Singh Nagoke was a self-styled lieutenant general of the militant outfit Khalistan Commando Force.
2. Jagran is a Hindi term that refers to a Hindu religious programme that is typically held over a night involving devotional songs, prayers and rituals.

NOTES

EPILOGUE

1. 'Don't Lecture on Intolerance, PM Tells Cong, Rakes Up Anti-Sikh Riots', *Deccan Herald*, 2 November 2015; https://www.deccanherald.com/india/dont-lecture-intolerance-pm-tells-2158286
2. The Nanavati Commission was appointed by the Central Government to look into various aspects of the 1984 massacre, including its causes and course, lapses and dereliction in the adequacy of administrative measures.
3. Himanshi Matta was a fomer media officer at Amnesty International.
4. '1984 Anti-Sikh Riots: Delhi Court Acquits Former Congress MP Sajjan Kumar', *The Economic Times*, 21 September 2023; https://economictimes.indiatimes.com/news/india/1984-anti-sikh-massacre-delhi-court-acquits-former-congress-mp-sajjan-kumar/articleshow/103818996.cms?from=mdr
5. Hartosh Bal in a publication by The Sikh Forum, pp. 53, 54.
6. 'CBI Says Eyewitnesses Saw Jagdish Tytler Instigating Mob during 1984 Riots', NDTV, 9 January 2024; https://www.ndtv.com/india-news/cbi-says-eyewitnesses-saw-jagdish-tytler-instigating-mob-during-1984-massacre-4828970
7. Gurmukh Singh Nagoke was a Sikh militant from Khalistan Commando Force.
8. For the protection of privacy, the name of the survivor has been changed.
9. 'Human Rights Violations in Punjab: Use and Abuse of the Law', Amnesty International, 1991.
10. 'Human Rights Violations in Punjab: Use and Abuse of the Law', Amnesty International, 1991.
11. For the protection of privacy, the name of the survivor has been changed.
12. Ibid.

13 Citizens for Democracy is an organization founded by Jayaprakash Narayan.
14 *Oppression in Punjab*, Hind Mazdoor Kisan Panchayat, 1985.
15 Human Rights Violations in 'Punjab: Use and Abuse of the Law,' Amnesty International, 1991.
16 Master Tara Singh was a prominent Sikh and political leader. He played a significant role in the Sikh community's political mobilization and advocated for Sikh rights and interests.
17 '1984 Riot Case Witness Seeks Amitabh Bachchan's Arrest', *The Times of India*, 29 October 2014; https://timesofindia.indiatimes.com/india/1984-riot-case-witness-seeks-amitabh-bachchans-arrest/articleshow/44965356.cms
18 For the protection of privacy, the name of the survivor has been changed.
19 For the protection of privacy, the name of the survivor has been changed.
20 Section 307 of the Indian Penal Code (IPC) defines the offense of attempting murder
21 For the protection of privacy, the name of the survivor has been changed.
22 Jarnail Singh, *I Accuse: The Anti Sikh Violence of 1984* (Penguin India, 2011), p 42.
23 For the protection of privacy, the name of the victim has been changed.
24 For the protection of the privacy, the name of the survior has been changed.
25 For the protection of privacy, the name of the survivor has been changed.

HarperCollins *Publishers* India

At HarperCollins India, we believe in telling the best stories and finding the widest readership for our books in every format possible. We started publishing in 1992; a great deal has changed since then, but what has remained constant is the passion with which our authors write their books, the love with which readers receive them, and the sheer joy and excitement that we as publishers feel in being a part of the publishing process.

Over the years, we've had the pleasure of publishing some of the finest writing from the subcontinent and around the world, including several award-winning titles and some of the biggest bestsellers in India's publishing history. But nothing has meant more to us than the fact that millions of people have read the books we published, and that somewhere, a book of ours might have made a difference.

As we look to the future, we go back to that one word—a word which has been a driving force for us all these years.

Read.

About the Author

Sanam Sutirath Wazir, a committed advocate for human rights from Jammu and Kashmir, is deeply engaged in documenting historical injustices and large-scale violence through oral history. He has successfully mobilized support from over half a million people across the world in advocating for justice for the victims of anti-Sikh massacres. His works, including 'An Era of Injustice for the 1984 Sikh Massacre', 'The 1984 Sikh Massacre as Witnessed by a 15-year-old' and 'The Continuing Injustice of the 1984 Sikh Massacre', are published by Amnesty International, etc.